A Life After Death

A Life After Death

The Struggle to Live After the Loss of a Child

Tristan and Jill Borland

RESOURCE *Publications* · Eugene, Oregon

A LIFE AFTER DEATH
The Struggle to Live After the Death of a Child

Resource Publications
An Imprint of Wipf and Stock Publishers
199 W. 8th Ave., Suite 3
Eugene, OR 97401

www.wipfandstock.com

PAPERBACK ISBN: 978-1-6667-1141-7
HARDCOVER ISBN: 978-1-6667-1142-4
EBOOK ISBN: 978-1-6667-1143-1

.   NOVEMBER 8, 2021 11:52 AM

Contents

Preface

ON MARCH 4, 2016, my daughter Maria died. She died suddenly in my arms when I was laying her down in her bed. Her heart shut down after being attacked by a common virus. She had no chronic illnesses. She was a happy and healthy almost four-year-old little girl when we lost her. We never saw it coming. In an instant she was gone, and our lives were devastated.

I am a pastor, but this isn't a pastoral book full of hopeful platitudes, nor is it a practical guide on how to overcome tragedy and grief. I haven't overcome. My family still grieves. This book is simply a memoir of our reflections during the months after Maria died. We have thought a lot about death, family, sorrow, and God these past few years, and now, over three years later, I still don't have much advice to give or answers to the perplexing questions raised by the death of a child. All we can offer are these honest writings in the hope that someone may find them helpful.

❋

Most of these reflections are ordered sequentially from the time Maria died. The majority of the reflections were written by me, Tristan. The reflections written by my wife Jill have been noted.

Preface

To Jill,

You are stronger and purer than you know. Your beauty grows deeper despite your pain.

To Jovi, Tana, Sadie, Lucy, and Elijah,

You remind us of joy every day. Many years from now I hope you read these words and remember your sister. On that day you may see a glimpse of the burden that we have tried to shield you from having to carry. I'm sure her death has affected your lives in ways that none of us can know, but I hope you have discovered much joy and grace along the way. May your lives be filled with wonder and delight.

To Maria,

You were beautiful. We miss you.

1

Six Months Later

TOMORROW MARKS SIX MONTHS SINCE the worst day of our lives. Even half a year later, we still have a hard time grasping what happened. Life has become more routine and tolerable. We have moments of joy and hope. But six months later we still find ourselves asking, "Did that really happen?"

We see reminders of Maria constantly, and her image often flashes across our minds. She's not really gone, is she? It's a daily struggle to reconcile the shock of losing her with the necessary calling to continue to live. We're getting better at living, but the shock remains. We still find ourselves looking for her. We still struggle to believe what happened.

You never know when the worst day of your life will come. There was no warning; no time to prepare my heart or my family for that devastating moment. Does tragedy always happen this way? It may sound obvious to others that calamity comes unannounced. I suppose that is the way most tragedies happen. Tragedy doesn't give you two weeks' notice that it will be coming to destroy your life. It makes sense in theory that tragedy comes without warning, but when it comes, theories are worthless. I believed the concept that "you are never guaranteed tomorrow," but I could never have fathomed on that day that it would be Maria's last.

Six months later, I am still dazed by the normalcy of the day she died. It was just a normal day. I went to my office in the morning. I had an appointment, and I finished preparing for weekend services. I took our older two daughters to a neighboring town in the afternoon to pick up a few things for work. We stopped to visit a young man I had been mentoring who was in rehab. We came home and ate dinner. We sat at the kitchen table and played a game. A normal day. A good day.

Maria had been a little sick and lethargic. She lay on the couch while the rest of the family ate and played. She asked me to take her to bed. I took a quick break from the game. I picked her up in my arms and carried her. As I laid her down on her bed she gasped, and her eyes rolled back. I screamed out for Jill. I didn't know it at that time, but her heart had stopped beating.

Jill bravely took action.

911.

CPR.

First responders.

Screaming.

Frantic phone calls for people to come watch our girls.

Chaos.

Weeping as this shocking reality began to sink into my bones that my little girl was gone.

Holding her body.

Then they take her.

Everything is silent except the sound of our wailing.

An hour earlier we had been playing a game. I still cannot comprehend it. It still doesn't seem real.

2

Cause of Death

WE WAITED FOUR WEEKS FOR the coroner's report on Maria's official cause of death. The coroner said that Maria died of myocarditis. Maria had caught an influenza virus that for some reason migrated to her heart and caused this condition. Myocarditis causes inflammation and damage to the heart tissue which is what ultimately led to her death. In my brief research, I keep coming across words like, "extremely rare" and "uncommon." Most cases of myocarditis present no symptoms. Even if it is detected, there is little that physicians can do.

On one hand, it was helpful to get this news. We now know why Maria died. Well, we at least know the medical condition that caused her death. I don't think I'll ever really know why. Why her? Why didn't her body fight off a common virus? Why is she the "extremely rare" case? Why would God allow her to be taken? The coroner's report can't answer the bigger questions.

3

Spunky Maria

MARIA WAS THE STRONGEST WILLED of our children. Jovi, our oldest daughter, has been obedient since the day she was born. Actually, she was obedient even before she was born. When Jill and I were eagerly anticipating her birth, we thought it would be great if she arrived on Monday, June 2, about one week before the due date. Sure enough, Jovi was born the day we had hoped for, right on time.

Maria was a different story. She arrived on her own terms, a week after her due date. Jill was at her parent's house when she went into labor. I was at work. Jill's aunt drove her to the hospital, and I drove the forty-five miles to the hospital as quickly as I could.

I found Jill in a tiny examination room already far into labor. She was there by herself and in significant pain. There was no room in the inn on the day Maria arrived. A lot of babies had just been born in that small hospital, and all the delivery rooms were full. I went and found a nurse to check on Jill. I told her that Jill's labor had been quick for her first two babies and that somebody needed to check on her as soon as possible. The nurse gave me a look that said, "relax, you panicky husband," but she appeased me and went to check on Jill. Sure enough, Jill was fully dilated and ready to start pushing. There was no time for an epidural; they rushed us into a room that had just opened. Thirty minutes later, Maria was born.

Maria was strong from the start. She kind of had to be because she was born into a busy family. She was the third daughter born in under four years, and her little sister Sadie arrived just seventeen months later. When you're the third of four daughters, all under the age of six, you must speak up or get lost in the mix. Maria was never afraid to speak up. She was tough and spoke her mind.

The summer before Maria died, Jill and I had the opportunity to take a ten-day sabbatical in Oxford, England. We have never been gone for so long from our daughters. My parents agreed to stay with the girls while we were gone. The evening before we left, I snuggled with Maria at bedtime and said, "Maria, I'm sure going to miss you while we're gone."

"I'm going to miss you too, Daddy."

"But we'll be back before you know it. And you will have lots of fun with Papa and Nene (my parents) and your uncles and aunts. You won't miss us too much."

She smiled. She wasn't very sad to see us go. Grandparents, uncles, and aunts can be lots of fun, and Maria loved to spend time with hers.

"Maria, are you going to be a good girl for Papa and Nene while we are in England?"

She paused and thought about it. "No," she said matter-of-factly. "I'm going to tell Nene, 'No!'"

I think Maria inherited some of her strong-willed nature from her grandma. She saw a conflict coming, and that spunky little girl was already preparing to be defiant.

I wanted to burst out laughing, but I did my fatherly duty. Hiding my smirk, I sternly said, "You better be a good girl for them while we are gone." She laughed at this. I laughed too, and we continued our bedtime ritual of snuggling and talking. Maria was always sweetest at bedtime knowing she could stay up a little later if she charmed her daddy with her sweetness. It worked that night.

Maria was true to her word. We called my parents from London, and they told me how Maria had disobeyed them, locked the door to her bedroom, and refused to let them in. My dad had to take the door off its hinges to get her out of the room.

I couldn't help but laugh as they told the story. Lots of children have moments of disobedience. Maria was just honest enough to warn us ahead of time. She was strong, and she spoke her mind. I miss her honesty and our snuggles at bedtime.

4

Good Friday?

(Three Weeks)

THIS FRIDAY IS GOOD FRIDAY, the day we remember Christ's passion, suffering, crucifixion, and death. How can we call this horrific day "Good"? Why do we celebrate the brutal killing of our Lord as one of our most sacred days of worship? At the center of the Christian faith are unexpected and seemingly contradictory images. We believe in an Almighty God who entered human history not to assert his power, but to die. Our most sacred symbol is the cross, an ancient and cruel method of execution. We believe that the way to find life is to take up our crosses, die to ourselves, and follow our Lord. We believe that in Christ's death, salvation and redemption are made manifest. All are unexpected and seemingly contradictory images.

This Good Friday will mark three weeks since the sudden death of Maria. Our lives are overwhelmed with unexpected and contradictory images. Three weeks ago, she was healthy, happy, and full of life. Three days later she breathed her last breath, and we held her lifeless body. How could this precious little girl that we loved so much really be gone? Every day we encounter heartbreaking reminders of her absence. Her clothes hang in her closet unworn. Favorite toys remain on the shelf. A bedroom is now empty.

No more hugs, tickles, playing, or dancing. Only silence, loss, and heartache remain.

How do we make sense of Maria's death? I really don't know. I don't have any easy or simple answers. The pain and shock are still too great. The only consolation I have is in the suffering and death of Jesus. Is God truly a God who enters into our suffering? Does his death really bring salvation and hope? Will death and meaninglessness have the final word, or will life and the resurrection one day conquer all? The only thing I hold onto in the midst of our suffering is that the horror of the cross is followed by the hope of the empty tomb. The darkness and sorrow of Friday is not the end of his story or our story. The sorrow is overwhelming, but it is not without hope.

❃

Three years, ten months, and two days. The time that Maria was given on earth.

A life cut short.

So much left undone.

So many dreams unfulfilled.

Each day we are haunted by the anticipation of plans that will never be completed. She was saving money to buy a doll. Her coins sit unused in her piggy bank. She was so excited to hold her new baby sister. Lucy was born one week to the day after Maria's death.

I was cleaning up my garage a few days ago, putting away Christmas decorations, and cleaning up clutter. I had to store away the bike that I was teaching her to ride four days before she died. She never got past training wheels.

There was a show on television last night. A father was walking his daughter down the aisle. He said she was beautiful and that he was so proud of her. I had to shut it off. I couldn't take it.

Maria loved one dance outfit more than her other clothes, but it was hard for her to take it off quickly and that caused problems for a little girl newly potty trained. She had a couple of accidents while wearing the outfit, so we took it away from her for a few weeks. She began to do much better going to the potty, and we promised her that she could wear her dance outfit soon. We buried her in it the next week.

So much left undone.

So many dreams unfulfilled.

Thirty-seven years, five months, and fourteen days. That's my current mark. Oh, how much of that I have wasted! Far too many days spent on selfish pursuits. How many days remain to love my wife, to raise my four living daughters, to carry my cross? Whatever my final number, I'm sure some will say "a life cut short." Are all lives cut short? Does everyone leave uncompleted plans and unfulfilled dreams?

Thirty-three years, they say he lived. His life was cut short. So much seemingly left undone. A kingdom unestablished. Cowardly friends in hiding. A body scourged. A mission incomplete. Can redemption really come to a life cut short?

5

Holy Saturday

(Three Weeks)

HOLY SATURDAY.

He descended to the dead.

The grave.

Silence.

Jill and I walked through the cemetery on Wednesday. It was a beautiful day for March in Minnesota. Sunshine and a cool breeze. Signs of an early spring.

We walked slowly. We talked softly. We stopped and wept where she is buried. There is no grave marker yet to indicate where her body now lies. Only dirt. We were surprised to find a rose left at this now sacred plot of ground. I have never cared about flowers, but that single rose touched us. A reminder of her beauty. A recognition that others remember her life and our pain.

Some might think our walk peaceful. But these quiet and serene grounds mock us with loathsome silence.

Jill and I are both quiet and reflective people by nature, but our life together is not a quiet one. We have had five daughters in less than eight years, and babies and young children bring noise, clutter, and chaos with them. I have already been interrupted many times this morning as I write this reflection. Jill is sleeping after being up with Lucy last night. I have had to stop and remind Sadie several times to be quiet and not to disturb her resting mother or her baby sister. Sadie has only two volumes: happy loud and angry loud.

Another pause.

Baby Lucy is awake, and I'm trying to calm her and buy Jill a little more time of rest. It's almost never quiet in our house. Four weeks ago, Jill and I would have casually joked about the craziness of our family. We coveted those rare moments when just the two of us could take a short break from the activity and noise of our children. We loved to go for peaceful walks. But now the silence left by the one who is no longer with us echoes wherever we go. We hear that silence over the cries of our newborn, over the demands of our toddler, over the play and laughter of our two oldest girls. An all-pervasive silence left by the one we laid in the ground.

6

Easter Sunday
(Three Weeks)

EASTER SUNDAY.

He is risen.

There is hope, but I'm having a hard time celebrating.

I believe.

Lord, help my unbelief.

I've been thinking about Thomas today. After Jesus had risen, the other disciples told Thomas that they had "seen the Lord." Thomas refused to accept this until he could touch Jesus' hands and feel his side. We call him "Doubting Thomas" because he didn't believe their report. The news was too good to be true. He wanted to touch and experience Jesus' resurrected body with his own hands. He couldn't believe until he saw, touched, and embraced the risen Lord. I don't find fault with Thomas. Is touching the risen Lord too much to ask when confronted with such an unbelievable claim?

When we first had children, we never let them sleep in our bed. We were disciplined parents who maintained routines and boundaries. We followed the rule-books for raising children. Bedtimes and sleeping arrangements were strictly enforced. But by the time daughters three and four came along, we were tired and worn out. Our older girls, Jovi and Tana, maintained consistent routines, but when Sadie was born only seventeen months after Maria, we threw out the rule-books and just tried to survive. Often when Jill was tending to newborn Sadie, Maria would come into our room at night crying. Rather than getting my lazy self out of bed and carrying her all the way back to her bedroom, I would usually just throw open the covers, and she would climb in. No matter how fussy she was, she would fall asleep within a few seconds of snuggling with me in my bed.

When she did sleep in our bed, Maria liked to sleep right up against me. She liked to have as much of her body in contact with my body as possible. The night before she died, her fever had broken, but she was still restless. She fussed, so I let her snuggle up next to me. She fell asleep immediately. She snuggled half the night with me and half the night with Jill. I'm so glad we let her sleep with us. Who would have known it was her last night?

The New Testament clearly teaches bodily resurrection. Thomas wasn't satisfied with his fond memories of Jesus. He didn't want to see a vision of Jesus or to talk with his ghost. He wasn't hoping for a mystical spiritual encounter. He wanted to embrace his Lord in the flesh. He wanted him back. In his body. He wanted to touch him.

Please don't tell me that Maria will "live on in our memories." This phrase brings me no comfort. Yes, I have my memories. It is hard for me to think about anything other than Maria in my grief. Share your memories of her with me. I need to hear your stories of her. I want to remember her. But please do not pretend that these memories are somehow equivalent to her life. They are only glimpses of the life that is now gone. Memories fade. Visions have no substance. Dreams do not last.

We so desperately want to touch Maria again. To smell her. To hold her. Our bodies long to have her spirit-filled body back with us. I want to feel her warm, skinny, sleeping body snuggled against mine at night. I want to hear her squeaky little voice telling her silly jokes and stories. I want to watch her dance and twirl in her favorite princess dresses. I want to feel her tiny little arms squeeze my neck. I want to tickle her in all those little places she loved to be tickled. I want her. Not a memory. Not a vision. Not a dream. Like Thomas I can't be satisfied with anything less than life fully restored. I've never longed for resurrection so badly in my life, but like Thomas, I'm having a hard time believing. It sounds too good to be true. But if the Father can raise Jesus . . . well, maybe someday.

7

A Life After Death

(One Month)

HOW DO WE SCHEDULE A FUNERAL for our three-year-old daughter when Jill is nine months pregnant? This is one of the many disorienting questions we faced in the days following Maria's death. Jill was pregnant with our fifth daughter. We set Maria's funeral for March 12, Jill's due date. Jill's water broke about 2:00 a.m. on the morning of March 11. The first message I sent from the hospital telling the news of our coming baby wasn't to our parents or siblings. I didn't call our children or our close friends to report the good tidings. I contacted our funeral director. We needed to postpone the funeral. Even our good news was tainted by death.

Our family had been greatly anticipating the arrival of our fifth daughter. All of us were excited to meet, hold, and welcome her to our family. Maria was the most excited. She would be a "big sister" this time. She was barely a toddler when Sadie was born, so she had no recollection of her birth. She would be able to hold this baby and help her mommy since she was finally becoming a "big girl." This was her chance. Every day she asked when the baby would be born so that she could hold her. She was so excited.

All excitement ceased when she died. I felt no joy going to the hospital that morning. Only fear and sorrow. We were about to receive and welcome our fifth daughter, but how could we embrace this new gift of life while our little Maria lay lifeless awaiting her final resting place?

Jill has had relatively short labors and deliveries. The longest previous labor was eight hours. This fifth labor dragged on through the night and morning and into the afternoon. Jill's body was still in shock from the tragedy. Maybe the baby was hesitant to leave the comfort and peace of the womb and enter our darkness and despair. Her labor slowly progressed. I began silently watching the clock. As evening approached, I knew that it was only a few hours until the time when Maria died exactly one week earlier. I dreaded that hour.

Lucy Faith was born 4:52 p.m. on March 11. Jill held her precious new baby. I tried to smile. I knew that she was a gift. I knew that she would be a blessing to our family, but I felt no joy. The best emotion I could muster was relief to see that she was healthy and to see my wife bonding with her newborn child.

I think I am a typical father and Jill a typical mother when it comes to our babies. I distinctly remember the births of each of our girls. The miracle of new life is glorious. However, it takes me a while to bond with the newborns. Jill, on the other hand, has bonded with each of our babies for nine months of pregnancy carrying them inside of her before they are born. I find that I'm much more useful giving my attention to Jill and our older girls when a new child arrives.

As Jill was nestling Lucy and continuing to build their already deep bond, my mind went instantly to our other girls: Jovi, Tana, Maria, and Sadie. Maria . . .

"Oh Maria, how can you really be gone? I remember your birth right here in this hospital. I remember holding you. I remember how excited your sisters were to come and meet you. I remember bringing you here seventeen months later when Sadie was born. I remember how excited you were to come here on this day to meet this precious little sister that your mommy now holds. I remember . . ." Each memory a stabbing wound on what should have been a glorious day.

I wept and held Jill. We wept and held Lucy. The nurses cried with us as they faithfully carried out their duties.

Lucy Faith. We didn't have any profound reason for giving her this name. It just sounded good to us a few months ago when we decided on it. Faith. Do I still have faith? I'm trying.

C.S. Lewis says, "Faith . . . is the art of holding on to things your reason has once accepted, in spite of your changing moods. For moods will change, whatever view your reason takes."[1] My moods have not just changed. They have been ravaged. On good days, I feel numb. On bad days, it's hard to get out of bed. Having a newborn forces us to get out of bed and face life no matter how much we don't want to. Perhaps the best grace Lucy has given us is demanding that we keep living, but I feel little joy in it. Yet, Lewis's words remind me that my joylessness is the result of my emotions being brutally assaulted by tragedy. What does reason remind me? What does faith declare? Reason reminds me that I will come to love Lucy like I love Maria and my other daughters. Faith whispers that joy will return to our home someday. I can barely hear it through our sorrow, but, occasionally, I detect its still small voice.

Lucy is one month old today. I don't normally pay much attention to the monthly milestones of our babies. I don't think I would have noticed today, but last week marked a month since Maria died. Lucy was born one week later. Thus, I remembered that she is one month old today. Will Lucy's life always be overshadowed by Maria's death? Each of Lucy's birthdays will mark another year of her life and another year since Maria's death. Seven days before each celebration of Lucy, we will stop and grieve the death of the sister she never met.

I know that I don't love Maria more than my other children. She was precious, but all my daughters are precious. I did not love her more than her sisters when she was alive. My love has not

1. Lewis, *Mere Christianity*, 71.

made her more special than my other girls. It is her death that has singled her out. In dying she is now set apart in my heart.

All my girls have birthdays. Only she has a date marking her death.

All my girls were bundled up, brought home from the hospital, and welcomed into our family. Only she was clothed for a final time and laid in the ground.

All my girls have birth certificates. Only she has a grave.

And I think of poor little Lucy. She is the only one of our five daughters who was not welcomed into a home of celebration. She came home to a house of mourning. She attended her first funeral two days later. She is familiar with the sound of weeping from inside and outside of the womb. Can she sense that her parents are heartbroken? Is she aware that every time I look at her I think about her sister? Will the celebration of her life always be overshadowed by Maria's death?

I take some consolation that Lucy is blissfully unaware. She is a baby. She will never have to understand nor experience the weight of our loss. As we get to know her as she grows, I am sure there will be many moments of joy and delight. She will develop a personality that will be uniquely her. She will be treasured in her own way. I see this in all my girls. Tana is distinctly Tana-like. Maria was uniquely Maria. And Lucy will soon be Lucy in her own way. She will be more than just the child born in the wake of her sister's death. She will be cherished and beautiful and good. But her life will be marked by Maria's death. All our lives will.

Lucy will be far more than just a sorrowful reminder. I look forward to watching her grow. I look forward to getting to know her. I look forward to seeing her for who she is instead of only seeing a reminder of Maria.

8

Crying Over Unspilled Milk
(One Month)

GRIEF SNEAKS UP IN ALL the little things. There are so many subtle reminders of Maria's absence. Daily unexpected moments that pierce our hearts. A couple of weeks ago I took our older two girls out hiking. It was muddy out, so I helped them put on their boots. Sitting among all the other shoes were Maria's boots, and a stabbing pain comes to my heart. How many times had I helped her take those boots off after she had put them on the wrong feet? She was still working on distinguishing her right foot from her left. Her boots are now empty. No little feet to wear them.

I was getting dinner ready the other night. I grabbed six plates out of the cupboard. There are still six in our family, right? As I filled each plate and brought them to the table, I realized I had an extra plate. Lucy isn't eating yet. There are only five of us at the table. There is an empty chair.

Maria was a milk drinker. Our older girls don't like milk. Our family would typically go through two gallons every week. These past few weeks we've been consuming less than a gallon a week. How much did that skinny little girl drink? She must have drunk a lot, and to be honest she spilled a lot too. Jill and I often bemoaned the fact that we averaged at least two spills every day as a family.

There are so many messes to clean up with all these little girls, but lately there are fewer spills. Less messes. Extra milk in the fridge. Simple reminders that pierce our hearts again and again. And there will be more subtle reminders today, tomorrow, and every day that will sneak up on us. All those little empty spaces that were once filled by our little girl.

9

A Larger Story
(Five Weeks)

IT'S BEEN HARD FOR ME to pay attention to news and current events. The rest of the world seems insignificant compared to the death of our daughter, but a tragic news story did catch my attention the week after Maria died. Four Missionaries of Charity were murdered in Yemen by members of ISIS the same day that Maria died. These faithful women operated a home for the elderly where they took care of the sick and needy. The four missionaries were among sixteen people seized, bound, and executed in cold blood. What senseless evil! Mother Teresa and her missionaries have always been ambassadors of compassion and mercy, so to hear that four of them were struck down in such heartless violence is shocking and disturbing.

But, this story had a surprising effect on me. It momentarily took me out of my personal loss and focused me on the sufferings of my brothers and sisters in Christ around the world. On the same day that Maria died, these four servants of Christ lost their lives too. This story does not bring me comfort. It does not lessen my grief, but it does give context to our suffering. We are not the only ones who have lost. We are not alone in our pain. Maria's death is not the only story of suffering. It is our story, but it is just one chapter of a much greater saga. The way of Christians has always been the way of the cross. We are carrying our cross. Others are carrying theirs. We are trying to be faithful in the role we must play, but we are just a small part of a larger story.

10

Not an Angel

(Six Weeks)

A FEW PEOPLE HAVE TRIED to console me with statements like, "Maria is now an angel in heaven." I don't agree with this assessment of the afterlife. I don't believe that humans become angels when they die, but I understand people's attempts to comfort me. They just don't know what to say. I get it. I don't know what to say either. Most people haven't given much thought to the state of the soul after death. I have thought a lot about this issue, not just since Maria died, but for years. "Maria is an angel" sounds nice, but I don't find much comfort in it. Statements like, "she's dancing in heaven, she's at peace, she's an angel now, etc." seem more like sentimental wishes than careful considerations of the afterlife. I don't find wishful thinking helpful. I do believe in the afterlife, but there is a lot that I don't know.

Here is what goes through my mind every time someone tells me, "Maria is now an angel." I think, "Huh, you think Maria is an angel? You must not have known my daughter. She is no angel!"

I told this to Jill a week after Maria died. It made us both laugh. We haven't laughed much lately. The irony of people saying Maria is an angel, while knowing how far from an angel Maria actually was, put smiles on our faces. Maria was certainly no angel.

Maria was the toughest and least compassionate of our girls. She wanted to do things her way, and when she didn't get what she wanted, she was quick to let us know. She was the slowest to smile and quickest to anger in our house. When she was about 2 ½ years old, I seriously worried about her stubbornness and lack of empathy. On Labor Day 2015, I dropped a fifteen-pound Pack-in-Play from a six-foot shelf directly on my big toe. It hurt bad, and I screamed out in pain (my toe later turned black-and-blue and my toenail eventually fell off). I iced my toe that night and thought I may have broken it.

The next day, Maria came up to me and said, "Daddy, does your toe still hurt?" I was touched by her tenderness and concern. I said, "Yes, Maria, my toe still hurts." She immediately looked down, lifted up her leg, and stomped on my foot as hard as she could. She looked up at me with her pretty blue eyes to see what I would do.

I was shocked! Thankfully, she was a tiny little girl who couldn't hurt me if she wanted to, and she had misjudged where I was injured and stomped the wrong foot. It didn't hurt my toe, but it injured my soul. I was wounded as a father. Was my precious little girl intentionally trying to hurt me? Does my daughter have no empathy? I said, "Maria! What are you doing?" She shrugged her shoulders, realized her stomping didn't hurt my toe, and went back to playing. Later that day I asked Jill, "Does Maria have no compassion? Was she really trying to hurt me? What is wrong with her?" Jill calmly responded, "I think Maria is trying to figure out the law of cause and effect. She knew you were injured and was trying to figure out how bad it was." That's when I knew how different each of our daughters is. Jovi is so empathetic she would have cried just because her daddy was hurting. Maria preferred to test the limits of my pain. Like I said, she was no angel, but none of our children are perfect. Jovi is full of grace and kindness, but she struggles to be courageous. Maria was brave but stubborn. Each of our children has virtues. Each has vices.

As Maria grew through the toddler stage and into her third year, she did become sweeter and kinder. But, she was still tough and had a long way to go. We taught her about God, and I believe she was beginning to grow in his grace. I trust she is redeemed, but she was far from perfect when she died. She certainly was no angel.

11

Where Her Body Lies

(Six Weeks)

JILL AND I WENT BACK to the cemetery today. Her headstone now marks where her body lies. Another reminder of the finality of death. Our little girl's name carved into stone reminds all who come here that her body will remain hidden until the end of the age. The date of her birth and the date of her death marking less than four years lived. A cross—the sign of suffering and hope. Words of faith. Her body will lie marked in this place until this stone turns to dust or until the end of all things. Her death will not come to an end in this world until all things end.

Maria was not only her body. I believe in the soul. But I only knew Maria through her body. The early Christians rejected the Gnostic belief that the body is evil and that only the soul is good. Death is not to be glorified as if it somehow sets the soul free from the confines of the corrupted flesh. Creation is good. The body is sacred. Death is horrible. Everything within me revolts against it. The Christian hope is not to become disembodied spirits. It is the resurrection and the hope of all things made new. Physical things fully restored. A new creation. Death and evil destroyed. Imperishable, resurrected bodies. But until that Day, this is where her body lies.

12

Pictures – by Jill

(Seven Weeks)

THE FIRST FEW YEARS AFTER I married Tristan, I enjoyed meticulously scrapbooking our family pictures. I would take time to lay out our pictures, crop them, and arrange them with different colored paper and embellishments until they looked just right. It was a slow process that created a big mess, but I enjoyed making albums with each perfect page. As our children came along, scrapbooking was no longer practical. The more consumed I was with our girls, the less time I spent documenting our life together. I did try to complete one online scrapbook a year for our family. It's a lot simpler and easier doing it online. I knew that one day I would want to look back and remember all of these crazy days.

Tristan and I fit the typical parent stereotype. We have thousands of pictures and videos of Jovi, our first-born. We have hundreds of pictures and videos of Tana, our second-born. We have a few dozen random pictures and videos of Maria and Sadie. The more kids we had, the harder it was to document everything. We brought our cameras to special events and holidays, but while changing diapers, feeding kids, and dealing with the chaos, we would typically forget to use them. At best we would hastily snap a photo or take a couple short videos. I did do the obligatory "first haircut," "first-solid food," and "first birthday" pictures for each girl's baby book, but other than those few occasions, we just didn't document much.

A few months ago, I realized that we hadn't updated the girls' pictures that hang in our kitchen in over a year. We hadn't taken a good family picture in almost two years. I didn't worry too much about it. Our fifth daughter would be born soon, and we would just get a family picture after she arrived; all seven of us together. That family picture is no longer possible. We will never be all together in a photo.

Pictures and videos of Maria have become priceless to us. There will be no more new pictures. No more new videos. Someday soon we will have viewed all that there are of her. I wish we had taken more. So much of her life was never recorded or filmed. So much is missing.

Will I now remember to regularly get out the cameras? I don't know. Would it make a difference? Even if we had taken twice the number of pictures and videos, there would still be a finite number of Maria. Our pictures and videos of her are priceless, but could we ever have enough? Maria's death has made them invaluable, but they are no substitute for her. I wish I had more pictures. I wish I had more videos. But she is still gone. I want to document these precious days that we have, but I don't want to just watch our girls through a lens. I want to be present with my children. Videos and pictures remind us of Maria, but they are not her. I wish I had more than pictures and videos. I just wish I had her.

13

The Risk of Love

(Seven Weeks)

JILL AND I ARE HURT and broken, but we must keep loving. Guarding ourselves against future heartbreak just isn't an option. To stop loving would be to stop living. We can't stop loving each other or our other children, but love is risky. It has the potential to cause the deepest pain. The thought of losing Jill or another child is terrifying, and I now know how quickly it can happen. Love is not safe.

But, what is the alternative? To close off our hearts? To protect ourselves so that we never get hurt again? Should we live the rest of our lives in isolation, giving ourselves to no one to avoid the potential of losing more people we love? Not only is this option not practical, it is the way of death. To stop loving and live only for self-protection is to stop living. Love is risky. Give your heart away and it will be broken, but there is no other good option. The way of love is painful, but it's the way we must keep living.

14

Talking to Strangers

(Eight Weeks)

WHAT DO I SAY TO STRANGERS? I like people. I usually enjoy talking with others, but since Maria's death I don't always know what to say. When people see our family in public, they say things like, "Wow, four girls! You have your hands full!" or "Four girls! Are you going to keep trying until you get a boy?" I used to laugh and chat with people after such comments. Now, I find myself tongue-tied. Should I say, "Well, actually we have five daughters, but our third daughter recently died." Most people at the grocery store aren't prepared for that conversation. I don't blame them. They are just trying to be friendly. They don't know about our loss.

I don't want to confront strangers with the harshness of our family's tragedy, nor do I want to ignore the reality of our daughter who isn't here anymore. A family of six is a large and peculiar sight to many in our culture. People like to make comments, especially about us having all girls. I usually just smile and nod thinking to myself, "We should be a family of seven, but one is no longer here. Six may seem huge to you. It feels incomplete to us. You may think we are odd. We should be even more odd."

"Trying until I get a boy?" Just to be clear, I'd much rather have Maria back than have a son.

A few weeks ago, I had to do some shopping in a neighboring town. I took baby Lucy with me to give Jill a break. As soon as I got to the store, Lucy started crying. I pulled her out of her car seat and tried to manage bouncing her in one arm while pulling a cart and trying to keep a pacifier in her mouth with the other. A young woman said, "Ah, what a cute baby! Is she your first?"

"No, she's our fifth daughter."

"Holy $#%! Did you have them all on purpose?"

I just stared at her without smiling. She could tell I was not amused. She said something like, "Well, good for you guys. Way to go!" and walked away awkwardly.

"On purpose?" Do I have the power to give and take life? If I have learned anything in losing Maria it is how powerless I am.

There are other strangers who know who we are. My position and our tragedy keep us in the public eye. Every week I have encounters with people who I don't know who ask us about our family and speak about our loss. I am grateful for these conversations. I think some people are nervous about talking to us about Maria. If you are among those who worry about making us feel bad or causing us to cry by talking about her, don't worry. It's okay to talk to us. We do feel awful, and we cry often, but you aren't the cause. We're just glad you remember. We're glad you can speak to our sorrow. We're especially glad if you say her name.

I took my girls to the playground the other day. A few young boys said, "Hey Pastor Tristan." I didn't know them, but I talked to them for a few minutes, and we got acquainted. Then the younger boy, a first grader, came over and sat beside me on a swing. He patted me on the back and said, "I know what's sad in your life. Your daughter died. She was three years old. She got sick."

I was touched by his courage and honesty. "You're right, buddy. You do know what's sad in my life. Thanks for remembering us."

15

Sacred Relics

(Eight Weeks)

JILL AND I HAVE NEVER cared much about stuff. We are not very materialistic. We intentionally try to live a simple life. We mostly care about relationships and our faith. Things have never been important to us. Until now. There are certain items in our home that have become priceless. Relics that she held; clothes she once wore, artifacts of plastic and fabric, and common objects made sacred by her life and by her death.

We have had five daughters in under eight years. Having all girls so close in age means that nearly everything is shared. Toys and outfits get handed from one girl to the next. They often share and trade their possessions so much that I can't keep track of who owns which doll, stuffed animal, or princess outfit. Clothes are also hard to keep track of. As soon as one girl grows out of an outfit the next one grows into it. Our family is the black hole for hand-me-down girl's clothing. Nice outfits given to our family end up tattered and threadbare by the time they make it through three or four of our daughters.

What clothes were distinctly Maria's? Which were her favorite toys? Everything blurs together.

Maria's things have remained untouched for nearly eight weeks. She and Tana had been sharing a room for over a year when Maria died. We moved Jovi and Tana back together immediately. We want them to be together through the grief.

Tuesday, Jill and I faced the heart-wrenching task of going through Maria's things. We have been dreading this day. What do we keep to remember her? What do we store for Sadie and Lucy? Piece by piece we went through her closet and drawers, weeping. Her pajamas. Her dresses. Her skirts. Two months ago, these were filled by our cherished daughter, now the clothes hang silently and empty. I held her clothes in my arms. I buried my tear-soaked face in them trying to detect her scent. I can't smell her anymore. Another reminder of her life that has faded. I held one pair of pajamas that I could distinctly picture her wearing. They are Dr. Seuss PJs, but I had never stopped to read the printed text. "Oh the Places You'll Go." Another dagger to my heart.

Three years and ten months of my daughter's life now consolidated into a box of sacred relics. Holy reminders of her life with us.

16

Birthday – by Jill

(Eight Weeks)

MAY 3, MARIA'S BIRTHDAY.

We have sensed the tension building in anticipation of this day. Lucy is the only one blissfully unaware of the strong undercurrents of grief in our home. How should we spend the day on which our daughter was to turn four? Do we keep ourselves busy and distracted, or do we plan for nothing other than reflection and sorrow? How do we engage our other children as we remember Maria's life?

I still feel as though we should be celebrating Maria's life today, not mourning her death. It is not difficult to imagine what we ought to be doing today. I can easily envision Maria's excitement and the grin on her face when she comes upstairs for breakfast and sees our "Happy Birthday" banner on the wall. She would ask, "Is it time for presents yet?" a dozen times as we eat breakfast and talk about the day ahead. Maria had wanted a real unicorn for her birthday. Tristan and I would drag out the time as long as possible before getting her presents out, probably teasing her that we decided to save her presents for next year. There would be laughter and cake and fun.

Instead, we wake up in tears but try our best to put on a brave face for the kids. My parents join us for the day. The girls paint rocks and help to pick out flowers to bring to the graveside. Tana requests a French braid in her hair since that is how Maria always wanted her hair done. Jovi insists on wearing her sunglasses upside down since that's how Maria often wore hers. We all wear a bit of yellow, her favorite color. Sadie struggles to understand the day. When we say we are going to Maria's graveside, Sadie says with a confused look on her face, "But Maria's with God." I try to explain that, yes, Maria is with God, but we were going to a special place to remember her sister.

On the car ride, Sadie begins to sing "Happy Birthday." She makes it two lines into the song. No one joins her.

Once there, we place the flowers and rocks by the stone marker. The sun shines while we stand there with hearts breaking. We try to sing songs that remind us of Maria.

As we return home, Sadie keeps repeating, "I want to see Maria. I want to talk to Maria. Please, Please, Pinky-Please!"

All I can say is, "I know, sweetie. So do I."

After supper, we take turns sharing some of our favorite things about Maria. There are finally a few smiles on our faces as we remember. How blessed we are to have had nearly four years with her. How daunting are the remaining years without her.

17

Four Years

(Eight Weeks)

FOUR YEARS AGO, SHE ENTERED our world on the same day her grandmother began cancer treatments. Her Grandma wouldn't be able to meet her or hold her for several months due to the chemo, a foreshadowing of sorrow and separation. Today we should be celebrating life and family, gathering, and giving gifts to honor her growth and health. But instead we come together to grieve our separation from her.

Like on most birthdays, we have gathered as a family. But there are no presents. Just flowers. No added candles to a cake to mark another year. Only a stone with fixed words and unchanging dates to remind us that there will be no more added candles. Flowers left where she lies that will soon fade as her life with us has faded.

There's a painful irony in that I took the day off from work. I took the day off because she is gone. If she were still alive, I would have worked. No need to take time off. It would have just been another birthday in the many birthdays we celebrate as a family. We would have had dinner and cake in the evening. There would have been gifts and laughter. Sadie would have cried because the gifts would have been for Maria instead of her, and she wouldn't understand this injustice. It would have been a typically joyful and chaotic family day, and I would have joined in after finishing my workday. But I stayed home today, not to be with her. I stayed because she is gone.

18

Beauty – by Jill

(Nine Weeks)

MARIA'S DEATH HAS BROUGHT A DARKNESS into my life that I have not known before. I've suffered heartaches, disappointments, and regrets in my past, but never this abyss that consumes me. I feel myself sinking deeper into the darkness of my soul. Some days I feel powerless to resist, and in my worst moments, I don't even want to try.

Tristan and I have discovered one thing that is able to penetrate this darkness. Beauty. I have little desire for fun or lightheartedness, but beauty can keep me from sinking to a place where I can no longer be reached. I crave beauty. I need to experience beauty in life. It's one of the only things keeping me going.

Even in sorrow, I still recognize the beauty of creation. The warmth of the sun on my skin, the smell of damp earth after a spring rain, the reawakening of plant life after the dormant winter, the vastness of the Minnesota sky. I recognize the beauty of music and the written word. I am grateful for those who have composed words that reflect what my heart has been crying; words that I have been unable to write. There is some small measure of healing that occurs when someone else can express those thoughts which are confused and jumbled in my mind.

I witness the beauty in love. My girls are beautiful—Jovi's sweet sensitivity to those around her, Tana's fun-loving spirit, Maria's strength and courage, Sadie's small voice shouting out, "I love you and we buddies!" Lucy's toothless baby grin—the depth of my love for them keeps me present and helps to soften my heart. Witnessing my husband's character and the support and love he offers me gives me strength.

I recognize the beauty of relationships and shared suffering. There have been key moments when friends have had the courage to join us in our grief, some who have experienced a loss like ours and some who have not. A few have been able to share their stories; all have offered their presence. They have listened. They have mourned with us and laughed with us and remembered with us. This road is a little less lonely when shared with these friends.

We serve a God that understands suffering. Christ did not spare himself from this dark side of humanity. I know that his suffering was good and necessary. Is it strange to call it beautiful? Beauty is what I most need, and despite the darkness and ugliness of this world, I still see beauty all around me.

19

Hurt

(Ten Weeks)

MANY WHO GO THROUGH GREAT LOSS become angry and blame God. That hasn't been my experience. I'm not angry with God. I know this world is a broken and sorrowful place. I am not naive, and I don't want to become bitter or jaded. I'm not angry with God, but I am hurt. I don't understand why he allowed this to happen.

I've been thinking about the story of Lazarus' death. Jesus delayed in going when he heard Lazarus was sick. By the time he arrived, Lazarus had died. Martha confronted Jesus, "If you had been here, my brother would not have died" (John 11:21, NRSV). I know this prayer well. "Where were you, Lord? If you had shown up that dreaded night, my little girl would still be alive. I'm not blaming you for causing her death. But I don't understand why you didn't show up and she died. Why were you silent that night? I don't understand."

Jesus responded to Martha, "Your brother will rise again . . . I am the resurrection and the life" (John 11:23, 25, NRSV). Martha trusted him, but she still didn't understand. That's where I am. Trying to trust while not understanding.

Then Lazarus' tomb was opened. An astounding miracle. Awe and wonder! The Messiah had won the day. But my Maria's grave remains unopened. No miracle. Only silence from God and the sound of our weeping by her grave.

Then I remember. Jesus wept. Those at Lazarus' tomb said, "See how he loved him!" (John 11:36, NRSV). Does the heart of God still weep with the brokenhearted?

The raising of Lazarus was a sign of things to come. The awe and wonder of that day brought temporary relief from the agony of death. Lazarus lived and then died again. His rising was only a delay before his inevitable death, and the Messiah who claimed to be the life was soon executed. If Maria's life had been saved, it would have been a temporary salvation. All of our lives lead to the same fateful demise.

Unless Lazarus's rising is a sign. Unless Jesus' tomb really is empty. Could it be that death is not the final word? Could He really be the resurrection and the life? Is death just the temporary state between life and abundant life? I don't understand, but I'm trying.

20

Living

(Twelve Weeks)

GRIEF MAKES ALL THE LITTLE THINGS DIFFICULT. Simple tasks that would have taken no planning or energy a few months ago have become arduous or exhausting. Everyday chores are much harder while grieving. Sorrow feels like sluggishness. It clouds our minds and slows our ability to function. But we must keep living. We will keep living. We continue to overcome simple hurdles like caring for our girls, cleaning, grocery shopping, attending church, etc. With each of these seemingly simple challenges comes a small victory.

We did the laundry.

Victory.

I went to the grocery store, faced the public, and bought a gallon of milk.

Victory.

Jill gave the girls baths.

Victory.

We survived another day.

Victory.

We continue to live.

Living

If these writings are the only glimpse a person has into our lives, it may appear that we are in a constant state of despair. That is not accurate. We are writing as a means to face our grief and to remember. We aren't documenting all the "normal" things of life. I am back to work. Jovi and Tana recently celebrated birthdays. Tana lost her first two teeth. Sadie continues to be loud and full of life. Lucy has been a good baby. Family has come to visit. Jill has been working on landscaping. I built some shelves in my garage. We've been reading a lot to the girls. We still laugh. We cry often. We keep living. But life is no longer the same. The "normal" never feels normal.

Living has become more manageable. What was unbearable in the weeks following Maria's death has become tolerable. Grief broke us and crippled us at first. It still does on certain days, but most days it is a cloud that darkens our life. Some days we have to face it, weep, and confront our sorrow. On the bad days, it can't be avoided, and it's hard to maintain a routine. On better days, it is still there. Most days, grief is silently lurking. It's always there in the background. We can laugh and play. We can experience joy with our girls, but grief never really leaves. It's part of our life now, but we are learning to live with it.

21

Anno Mortis Eius

(Three Months)

MARIA'S DEATH HAS BECOME the most impacting experience of my life. I have never faced anything that has so radically changed me in an instant. My faith, marriage, and fatherhood are probably more formative than Maria's death, but each of these have been gradual and ongoing in their impact. Faith is continual. I don't remember one distinct moment of conversion. My relationship with Jill has shaped me more than any other temporal relationship. Our wedding day was a big day, but it was just one big day among many important days in our life together. The births of our five daughters have been some of the greatest days of my life, but there have been five births; only one death. The day Maria died was cataclysmic. In one moment, our world was upended, and in the aftermath, nothing remains as it was before that day.

Her death has become the central reference point of my history. Several times each week I find myself mentioning her death. Even in casual conversation I say things like, "that happened a month before Maria died," or "we haven't done that since Maria died." I don't bring up her death to be morbid or depressing. I reference her death because everything changed the moment that we lost her. The people we were before March 4, 2016, were very different than the people we are today. Everything seems different since that day. Time passes more slowly now. I process information differently. I feel less at home in my own body. And as I experience these changes, I realize that our history has become divided into two distinct eras: before Maria died and anno mortis eius (in the year of her death). Reality changed forever that night.

But is this true or just my perception? I don't want to make Maria into an idol. Her death did not transform nature. It just revealed our fragility, our own lack of faith. Her death didn't upend the world, just our world.

In the sixth century, Christians began to reckon time to the incarnation. God has come to dwell among us, the central event in human history. By putting on flesh, God divided history into two eras. All that preceded the incarnation–Before Christ (BC). And every year since–Anno Domini (AD) which is Latin for "in the year of our Lord."

On the fourth day of March, in the two-thousand-and-sixteenth year of our Lord, our lives were changed forever. All the days of our lives before that day feel as if they occurred in an alternate history. Life was different then. Our time is now understood in light of anno mortis eius. Each day marks one more day since the day she died. This is the first year in the year of her death, but it also remains the year of our Lord. This era is not the final era. Her death defines our new reality, but so does his life.

22

Sadie

(Three Months)

OUR DAUGHTER SADIE IS ONLY 17 months younger than Maria.
Maria and Sadie are the closest in age and the two most boisterous
of our daughters. Every day Sadie says and does things that remind
us of Maria. She is forcing us to relive much of the last year of
Maria's life. She is a good and painful reminder of her big sister.

Maria was our hardest child to potty train. She finally got the
hang of it about a year ago. Now we are potty training Sadie, our
second hardest. I was trying to get Sadie to use the potty a few days
ago. I started to sing the silly "potty song" that I made up, but it got
stuck in the back of my throat. I sang that song hundreds of times
to Maria as she sat on the potty and did her silly dance while we
both waited for her to pee. We tried everything to get that girl to
use the potty, but true to her strong-willed self, Maria was going to
potty train on her own terms. So, I would sing my "potty song." She
would do her silly dance, and we would laugh and laugh. I couldn't
sing it to Sadie. The image of Maria flashed through my head. No
song. No silliness.

There has been a lot less dancing in our house. For years, our
evenings have been filled with music, frilly dresses, and lots of girls
twirling and dancing. I would sometimes join in playing the role

of Prince Charming to all my little princesses. It's been too painful these past months. We still put on music some nights, but I've noticed that even Jovi and Tana don't dance much anymore. They are getting older and are more self-conscious. I also think they feel the sadness and have a hard time finding the joy to twirl. Most nights Sadie still dances, and we try to smile at her beauty while hiding our tears as we think of how much she looks like her sister.

Each night at dinner, I ask if one of the girls would lead us in prayer, and each night Sadie eagerly volunteers. She folds her hands, bows her head, and prays the exact same thing every time. "Thank you, God, for this great day. Bless Jovi, Tana, Maria, and Sadie. Amen!"

And every night we say, "And?"

She immediately remembers and prays, "Oh, and Lucy too. Amen."

Thank God she forgets the baby and not Maria. But she is so young. Her memories will soon fade, and one day all that she will remember about Maria are the stories we tell her. I mourn for the loss of her closest sister. They were just starting to play together. They would have played a lot together at this stage of life. They would have fought a lot too; I'm not naive. Sadie now has two older sisters who often do things together without her and a baby sister who can't join her yet. So, she dances alone.

23

Calamity and the Face of God
(Three Months)

JILL AND I USED TO TALK about how fortunate our lives have been. We both grew up in faithful and loving families. Both sets of parents are still married. We have good relationships with our siblings and their spouses. Most of our family are committed Christians. We have always had work, and our needs have always been met. We've been loved well and have had a relatively easy and good life, until this year.

Jill's mother's cancer returned last spring. It was much more aggressive when it returned after being in remission for a few years. They had to harvest her stem cells, do heavy chemo treatments, and then reintroduce her stem cells. It was scary and she suffered a lot. Thankfully, she is recovering, and her tests look good so far.

While she was in Minneapolis receiving her treatments, one of the three workers on their family dairy farm had complications with appendicitis, was rushed to the hospital, and was unable to work for several weeks. So, my father-in-law had to stay and work on the farm while his wife was going through the cancer treatments. Then a terrible storm hit the farm, causing major damage. My father-in-law remarked that he was beginning to feel like Job.

Then Maria died. The greatest tragedy for our whole family. Jill and I are not the only ones who grieve. Grandparents, aunts, uncles, and cousins all lost her too. They share in the heartbreak.

On Monday, Jill's parents' house burned down, the house she grew up in. We no longer feel like our family has been blessed with ease and good fortune. Her dad's comparison to Job is starting to seem all too real.

Job is the book in the Old Testament that deals with theodicy (vindicating God's omnipotence and goodness despite the existence of evil and suffering in the world). Job suffered greatly. His friends showed up and met with him in his suffering, but after many long discussions and much pontificating, his friends were unable to adequately explain Job's plight. Job was faithful and just, and his friends provided no reason why such calamity had fallen upon him. Then, at the end of the book, God finally spoke, but even God did not give an answer for Job's suffering. God didn't give Job what he was looking for, but in speaking, God himself became Job's answer. Job was satisfied not because he received an explanation, but because he encountered God himself. We will never find sufficient answers for our suffering, but God transcends our questions.

We still have no answers for Maria's death. When designing a gravestone for her burial, the best we could come up with was a quote from C.S. Lewis' novel *Till We Have Faces*. In the book, the protagonist wrestles with the problem of evil and suffering and comes to the conclusion that there are no adequate answers. She had become bitter at the gods and demanded justice until she finally encountered the Lord face-to-face. Then she says, "I know now, Lord, why you utter no answers. You yourself are the answer. Before your face, questions die away."[1] This is the quote we had engraved on Maria's tombstone. It encapsulates how we think about her death. We have no answers. We will never understand, but God is still present. Why have all these things been allowed to happen? I don't know, but before his face we continue to trust without answers.

1. Lewis, *Till We Have Faces*, 308.

24

Sentimentality and the Afterlife

(Four Months)

WE DISCIPLINE OUR CHILDREN. There are times when we are strict with them because we love them and want to form their character in the right direction. Virtue leads to joy and vice leads to misery, so it is our duty to instill virtues and limit vices. We don't physically or emotionally abuse our children. We don't discipline out of anger. But we do discipline them; some more than others.

Jovi has never needed much discipline. She was so tender-hearted that even at a young age, if I scolded her, she would instantly burst into tears and seek forgiveness. As for my other girls . . . well, let's just say we've had to be more strict. It seems that from age two to age four, most of our girls go through a phase in which they need more than just scolding to learn to obey.

Sadie is currently going through this phase. She's usually a pretty good kid, but several times a week she will become angry and defiant. We will confront her and give her every chance to obey, but often she refuses to comply and stands her ground to make sure that we follow through with our promised discipline. Often the conversation goes like this, "Sadie, you did not obey your mommy. You need to say you are sorry."

She stands with her arms crossed defiantly.

"Sadie, I'm going to give you three seconds to apologize or you're going to get a spanking."

She continues to stand refusing to move.

3 . . . 2 . . . 1½ . . . 1 . . . you better get moving . . . "

She stands her ground refusing to budge.

"Ok, you're getting a spanking."

Immediate crying.

A quick swat on the bum.

More crying, and then she softens.

We snuggle. I explain again why I had to discipline her. She says she's sorry, and moments later everyone is happy again.

When Tana was three, I remember asking her what her bedtime routine was. She said, "I get my jammies on. I brush my teeth. We read a story. I get my last drink. We say a prayer. You tuck me in. I give hugs and kisses. I throw a fit. I get a spanking. I go to bed." She seriously listed a "spanking" among her evening rituals! I promise, we are not abusive parents. It was just a phase for her.

Maria received her fair share of spankings. She was our most defiant child. Not long after we lost Maria, I remembered an encounter we had less than a week before she died (but before she became sick). Jill had asked Maria to do something, and she very defiantly shouted at her mommy, "No!"

I spoke strongly and sternly, "You will not talk to your mother that way."

She looked at me, crossed her arms, stomped her foot, and defiantly grunted "No!" again.

I said, "Okay, little girl, you're going to get a spanking."

I took her to the bedroom, gave her a little swat on her bum. I don't think it hurt even a little bit. I tend to err on the side of being gentle, and she didn't soften. She stormed off on her own in anger. I gave her a few minutes to cool down and went to talk to her. I told her that she needed to go tell her mommy that she was sorry, but that stubborn little girl looked at me coldly, shouted, "No!" and pulled her covers over her head. I had to discipline her again, and this time she eventually softened. We snuggled. She apologized to

Jill, and everything was resolved for the evening. She died less than a week later.

I remembered this situation a few days after she died, and my heart sank. In my sentimental emotions I thought, "Why does one of my last memories of our time together have to be of me disciplining my little girl and her defying me? I just want to hold her and kiss her again. I just want to be with her again. Oh, I miss her so bad."

And then I had another thought. I disciplined her because I loved her, and she knew that. She really did know that. Even in her anger and stubbornness, she was never afraid of me. She was never afraid of Jill. She knew she was loved and secure partly because we did discipline her. And she knew that even when she defied us, there would always be tenderness, reconciliation, and security in the love of her parents. Sentimentality makes me think that I should have always given her ice cream and toys instead of the occasional punishment. Reality reminds me that we loved her enough that we were willing to discipline her.

There wasn't much laughter in our house in the weeks following Maria's death, but I remember one of the first times we laughed. Jovi, Tana, and I were talking about the afterlife. We were talking about what Maria might be experiencing. We said things like, "We've trusted her into God's hands. We don't really know much of what she is experiencing, but we have to trust God. And God is good." And then I threw out the question to my girls, "Do you think God has given Maria any spankings yet?" We all burst out in spontaneous laughter, partly because the question sounded ridiculous and partly because it seemed so true to the stubborn little girl that Maria is. And the more I've thought about it, the less ridiculous my question seems. I'd consider myself to be at least a mediocre loving father, and I disciplined Maria because I loved her. Wouldn't a perfect loving Father also want to lovingly discipline his children until they have grown to maturity? He disciplines me in love. Why wouldn't he with her? I know this is speculation. There's a lot we cannot and will not know about the afterlife from this side of the grave, but the more I think about our

Heavenly Father, the more I believe he will bring each one of us to completion even if it requires the occasional discipline.

I would give up everything to have Maria back, but if she were back, I would not give her everything. I wouldn't give her everything she wanted because it wouldn't be good for her. True joy comes from God, from growing in holiness and virtue, and from laying down one's own self for the good of others. I'm willing to guess that this is not just true for this life but for the next life as well.

I don't know what Maria is experiencing right now, but I hope it is more than mere pleasure and ease. I hope it's deeper. I hope she's really becoming holy and good. I hope she is being made complete, even if it isn't easy. Maybe God has even given her a few swats on the bum along the way, and if he has, I know he has done it in love. And if he has, I know that stubborn little girl deserved it.

25

Ten More Minutes

(Five Months)

I WOULD GIVE ALL OF my possessions to have ten more minutes with Maria. If we could just hold her again one more time. Oh, how I long for a last chance to tell her goodbye, to assure her of our love. To kiss her precious face. To weep with her and to tell her how sorry we are that we won't be with her. To pray with her one last time before entrusting her into the hands of God. She died so suddenly. There was no chance to say goodbye.

I can't imagine ever desiring anything as much as I desire just ten more minutes with her. There is nothing that I will ever want more than to be with her again. But it cannot be. It will not be. Facing the future is daunting because the thing that I want more than anything else is not possible. I know there will be happy times again, but I will always be longing for just ten more minutes.

26

The Babble of a Mortal

(Five Months)

YESTERDAY'S POST WAS A CRY in the darkness, but are my words true? My broken heart cries out in pain, but I must also use my head. My heart and my mind continue to wrestle to try to make sense of our loss.

Would ten more minutes with Maria really quench my desperate soul? Would I want just ten more minutes? Or ten more days? Then ten more years? Ten more decades? Ten more lifetimes? I would ask for more and more time until time would force love to become common, and I would take her for granted. In loss, the heart recognizes the desperate need for the beloved, but as time becomes indefinite, desperation diminishes. Neglect becomes inevitable. We beg for time only when time is gone.

Could I really express my love for Maria in ten minutes? If our life with her did not adequately assure her of our love, would a few rash and despairing words make a difference? She knew our love. She was secure in our arms. I would write countless words to declare our love for her if it would make a difference, but it wouldn't. She knew as much as an almost four-year-old could know. She knew she was loved. Words wouldn't have changed that.

Could I really prepare her to enter into the presence of God? Am I capable to mediate between her and the Holy? In my brokenness and selfishness, I know I am not capable. I realize how insufficient, powerless, and impure I am. I realize it more than ever in these dark and despairing days. I could not prepare her for what I do not know. My faith has not become sight. I could not lead her down the lonely path I have never journeyed. Only he can call her to himself. Only he can lead her.

There is great mystery in loss. I constantly find that my desires and understandings are veiled. I see glimpses of truth, but only glimpses. I cannot ask for endless time because I am mortal, and my time is finite. I cannot offer assurance of endless love because I do not know how to love well. I am still learning to love. I cannot give answers to my burning questions because my mind is incapable of grasping the Divine. Only God can lead her into the land of the holy where my footsteps have never traveled.

27

More Speculation on the Afterlife
(Seven Months)

MANY PEOPLE SPEAK TO ME about the afterlife with great confidence but not much clarity. They say things like, "We know Maria is in a better place. She is perfectly happy in heaven right now." I appreciate their attempt to encourage me. Most who make these statements are people of faith and have a genuine hope. Many have a greater faith than I do. I still have faith, but it feels weakened. I have enough to get me through today. That's the most I can muster. I have hope, but my hope is not simple. It contains sorrow and doubt. My hope is not sentimental, but it remains.

When I'm being honest, I ask a lot of questions, not as a cynic, but as one whose hope is not simple. I ask, "What do people mean when they say Maria is in heaven?" I think most people mean that she has arrived at her final destination with God, but this doesn't seem right. The Christian hope is not that we will one day leave our bodies behind and enter into an eternal spiritual existence. The creed declares our hope, "We believe in the resurrection of the body and the life everlasting." The resurrection. The body restored. Our hope is a real, physical, and eternal life, not a Gnostic, spiritual, euphoric state of the soul. Our hope is founded on the resurrection of Jesus. It is the hope that one day there will be a new heaven, a new earth, and new bodies. On that day, life will not just be restored, it will be glorified to a state of existence beyond all the beauty, goodness, and joy we experience now. On that day death will be swallowed up by life. But that day hasn't come yet, so we wait. I imagine Maria is waiting too.

My unsentimental hope asks, "What is Maria experiencing right now?" I honestly don't know. Is she dancing and twirling on the streets of gold? Some people say things like this. It sounds nice, but it doesn't help me. Why? Well, it sounds like bodily resurrection. It's hard to think about how a person can dance and twirl without a body. Since the resurrection hasn't happened yet, I just can't imagine what it means to dance and twirl. It also sounds like wishful thinking. It's what I would want to be true to make me feel better about Maria's death, but wanting something to be true does not make it so. Hope is not the same thing as wishful thinking. If I base my beliefs only on my desires, I am only fooling myself. I will not allow my emotions to dictate what I believe to be true, even about Maria. Hope must have a foundation in reality. Wishful thinking is the stuff of fantasy, not faith. I wish Maria never died. I wish she were still alive. I wish I was holding her right now. But wishes are just wishes. My hope about the afterlife cannot be based on what I want. It cannot be founded on what I wish to be true. My hope must be established on something substantial, and the one substantial hope I have is the resurrection of Jesus Christ. I agree with St. Paul. "If Christ has not been raised . . . your faith has been in vain" (1 Cor 15:14, NRSV). My hope is not in conjured up images of Maria dancing in the clouds. My hope is in the resurrection of Jesus. Don't misunderstand. I do believe in a real afterlife. I believe that Maria's soul still exists, but what that existence is like is more mysterious and less tangible than I can pretend to know.

My unsentimental hope also asks, "Is Maria perfected?" or "Has Maria arrived at her final state of rest?" I am referring here to the state of Maria's soul, not the resurrection of her body. Is she holy? Has she been made complete? Most Christians seem to assume that Maria and all other Christians who die are instantaneously perfected at death. They speculate that the dead are immediately glorified the moment after they breathe their last breath. Maybe that's possible. But I'm not sure it's what happens. Paul was confident that, "to be absent from the body" is "to be present with the Lord" (2 Cor 5:8, KJV), but does this imply that the soul is instantly matured and made perfect the moment one dies? In this life, maturation and transformation require discipline and struggle and grace and time, and I'm not convinced that one's journey into the afterlife is simple and easy. Maria was not even four years old when she died. She had a lifetime of learning and maturing ahead of her. It's hard to imagine that she would gain complete wisdom, maturation, and perfection in a mere moment. Certainly, she will not remain perpetually transfixed as an immature, almost four-year-old child for all of eternity, so how will she be made complete? I imagine she will continue to grow and be transformed, but I have no idea how or what that looks like beyond the grave. So much remains a mystery.

Here is what I do know. God is merciful. He is also terrifyingly holy. Who among us could stand before the LORD? If you casually think that standing before a perfect, holy, and all-powerful Deity will be a comforting experience, then I'd argue that you haven't given it much thought. The day she died, Maria was far from perfect. This is not a criticism; it's a statement of fact about nearly every Christian I know, including myself. Almost all of us continue to be selfish, sinful, immature, and unwise. We lack virtue and continue to struggle with vices.

For heaven to be heaven, many things within us must be changed. If we're honest, we should admit how far we are from reaching perfection and from being made complete. Imagine spending the rest of eternity with all the people in your community or church if everyone remains as they currently are forever. Would you be able to live in loving fellowship for five years? Or for a million years? Of course not! The sins and pride would eventually come to the surface, and it would definitely not be heaven. We all know that for eternity to be good our hearts need to be drastically changed first. We all need to be made complete.

Maria was far from being perfect, far from being complete when she died. Maybe she is now fully changed. Maybe she is still being changed. Maybe she is at peace. Maybe she is still struggling on her journey. Maybe speculating about what Maria is now experiencing is vanity. If her soul has left space and time, maybe words like "now" are meaningless. Maybe I don't know much. Maybe nobody really knows, except for God. Only God knows. I guess that's all I need to know.

28

Awkward – by Jill
(Five Months)

RIGHT ABOUT THE TIME that I was entering junior high, I became reserved and quiet. I preferred to be at home, preferred to blend into the crowd, and preferred to listen rather than speak. I struggled to initiate conversations with anyone other than those I knew well. As I grew and matured into adulthood, I learned how to better engage with others. I have come to enjoy hosting and getting to know new people. I am still an introvert, but I'm not as awkward as I used to be.

Since Maria's death, I find myself reverting back to my junior high years. I want to withdraw more than I want to engage. I find myself awkwardly not knowing what to say. I quickly ask questions because it's easier to listen than to talk. Maybe I notice my own awkwardness more than anyone else does. I hold people at arm's length more than I did before Maria's death. I'm so tired and relationships take a lot of work. I feel vulnerable. I'm still guarding this wound that is so easily reopened.

There are a few relationships that I continue to lean on, but even in those I feel vulnerable. I have little to give right now. I depend more heavily on a few friendships. I fear that others, people that I truly do love, will take my silence or my absence as coldness or indifference. I don't intend to be cold or indifferent. I still love people. I just rarely have the strength to show them. I don't want to remain superficial or distant, but I just can't talk about what is really going on in my heart. Please be patient with me in my awkwardness as I try to find my voice again.

29

Fingerprints

(Seven Months)

WE DISCOVERED A HOMEMADE ORNAMENT buried in the girls' closet a few days ago. Maria must have made it in Sunday School last December. It's strange to think that if she were still here, I would have most likely thrown it away. We accumulate lots of knickknacks and toys and end up tossing most of them. But this ornament is no worthless trinket. It is a sign of her life. It contains her fingerprints three months before she died; her last Christmas. I dread Christmas this year.

The ornament was sitting on my computer desk. Sadie was snuggling on my lap and saw it. "Daddy, I wanna bring dat to Maria? When will Maria be back from God?"

"It'll be a long time, Sweetie. A really long time."

"Are you sad, Daddy? You miss Maria, Daddy? I give you kisses and hugs. Dat will make you feel better."

"Thanks, sweet Sadie."

30

Young Love and Young Grief

(Seven Months)

WITH THE ARRIVAL OF AUTUMN and the busyness of a new school year, we have spent less time writing. I dabble with some words here and there, but it's difficult to find the energy to face our grief. Work and children keep us distracted. Maria's death no longer consumes every waking thought. Grief has not dissipated. It has just gone deeper.

I was recently thinking about the first time I met Jill. We met at the tail end of a six-month stint I spent in Brazil. A week before I moved back to the States, Jill showed up on a ten-day trip. Not only did I find her beautiful and sweet, but she also spoke fluent English which was very attractive to me at the time! After spending half of a year in a foreign country, the chance to get to know this Minnesota girl was more than exciting. I quickly found out that she was going to be moving back home for the summer. I had already taken a job in Minnesota for that summer, and we would be living within an hour of each other. I had one week left in Brazil, and I spent as much time as possible trying to get to know Jill and to win her over with my charms. Almost fourteen years, later she's still hanging out with me. I must have done something right.

Ah, young love! The emotions of attraction are intense in the early days of a relationship. I remember lying awake at night that first week just thinking about her and the potential of being with her. I remember the butterflies in my stomach when I talked with her. I remember scheming so that I could "coincidentally" spend time with her. The emotions of falling in love are strong. But I hesitate to call these emotions "love." If falling in love is truly love, it is a shallow version of it. I didn't really love Jill in those early days. I loved the idea of Jill. My heightened emotions of attraction drove me to pursue her, but I pursued her mostly for my own sake. Young love is powerful, but real love goes deeper.

My love for Jill has gone deeper. I no longer experience the same intensity and frequency of emotions as I did in those first days, and I'm glad that I don't. This may sound strange, but Hollywood has deceived us into thinking that intoxicating romantic feelings should last forever, but who could really live in a continual heightened state of romance? The sleepless nights, butterflies, and scheming must inevitably decrease. The intensity of young love must eventually settle down. But as young love settles, real love can grow deeper. Love becomes less about heightened emotional attraction and more about faithfulness, friendship, duty, children, and sacrifice.

When I first saw Jill, I dreamed about life with her. I was drawn to her and hoped she could improve my lonely existence. Now, I cannot imagine my life without her. She has become intricately entwined with who I am. I am no longer just autonomous Tristan. I am now the husband of Jill, characterized not by my individuality but by my commitment to love my wife and children. Our lives have become one. Jill's life has become so much a part of my life that it's hard to even remember what life was like when I was single. When I look at her now, I see the woman who has faithfully walked by my side. I see my friend who always patiently listens to my neurotic ramblings. I see the worker who sacrificially offers her energies to daily serve our family. I see the mother who bore our five daughters. I see my lover and my most intimate companion in suffering, whose heart was broken with mine the day we lost our little girl. My love has gone far deeper than romantic sentiment. The emotions of young love have faded, and in their place, a more substantive love has been forged.

Like love, grief has gone deeper with the passing of time. In the early days, the shock and despair of Maria's death were unmanageable. We wept constantly. We couldn't eat. We couldn't sleep. We could think of nothing other than her death. The intensity of our loss was all-consuming.

As days turned into weeks and weeks into months, some of the intensity of our grief has weakened. It had to. We couldn't survive otherwise. But as the intensity has weakened, our grief has gone deeper. I no longer think about Maria's death every moment of every day. Many of our normal routines have resumed. Yet, we are different now. Grief has sunk into our bones. It has changed us. Maria's death has become part of our identity. We are now "those parents whose little girl died." Her death is part of our identity. I'm having a harder time remembering what life was like before she died. I was a different person then. Our family was different then. Grief has gone deeper.

3 1

Thanksgiving

(Eight Months)

THANKSGIVING. A DAY FOR FAMILY AND GRATITUDE. Despite the inescapable absence at our table and the ever-present ache that will now be part of our holidays, I still have much to be thankful for. I don't feel thankful. It's hard to feel gratitude and sorrow at the same time. But I know I am blessed. This first Thanksgiving after her death, I feel broken, but I know I am also fortunate. I know that we have been loved well in the midst of our sorrow.

Today I am thankful for our community. I love our little town. Neighbors, friends, acquaintances, and strangers have supported us, grieved with us, and loved us. In the worst days of our lives, they flooded us with generosity. I am reminded of George Bailey in *It's a Wonderful Life*. In his moment of desperation, when he was on the verge of forfeiting his life, the grace of God showed up in the form of his community, and they saved him. They gave abundantly more than George could have ever imagined. Their grace was greater than his debt.

We live in a good community, and when a good community doesn't know what else to do, it gives. Nobody really knows what to do when a child dies. Everyone feels powerless. There is nothing that anyone can do to "fix" it, and since the people in our community couldn't fix our heartbreak, they just gave and gave and gave.

Money really doesn't mean much to me anymore, but the amount that was donated to our family was overwhelming. Tens of thousands of dollars were given; it was far above any costs that our family incurred in funeral expenses. The total was staggering. I would publicly disclose how much was given, but I am not going to because it's embarrassing. It was far too much, and while the money wasn't necessary, it is a sign of the great generosity of our community and friends. We were able to use much of what was given to setup some memorial funds and bless others in memory of Maria.

People prepared dozens of meals and fed us for months after Maria died. Not only did our church feed us and give to us, but the people from other local churches brought us meals for weeks. None of them attend my church. I don't even know many of them. But they gave. I think we still have a few Lutheran casseroles in our freezer!

I think of how our community bent over backwards for us in the immediate days following Maria's death. When she died, we faced two major complications in trying to schedule her funeral. The first complication was that Jill was nine months pregnant and could go into labor any day. The second was that the only building large enough to hold the crowd for Maria's funeral was our high school gymnasium. I talked to our school superintendent, and she graciously assured me that they would do whatever we needed. We scheduled visitation for Friday and the funeral for Saturday at the gym. It happened to be the end of the school's spring break. Volunteers and custodians set up hundreds of chairs, video equipment, a sound system and prepared all of the details. Musicians arranged their schedules and practiced. Friends and family traveled from hundreds of miles to be with us. Then, early Friday morning Jill went into labor. The visitation and funeral were immediately postponed. Friends and family all had to rearrange their schedules. Our school had to take down all of the chairs and audio/visual equipment to prepare for school on Monday. Then, they rearranged the school calendar and canceled events. They set everything back up in the gymnasium and re-prepared all the details to accommodate us for Maria's funeral. Our school, community, friends, and family stopped everything in order to serve us. Have I mentioned that I love our community?

I am also grateful for the body of Christ. Following a heated political season, I desire peace. I long to be a part of a community that transcends the quest for temporal power. A community that lovingly speaks truth rather than inflammatory rhetoric, that treats people as the sacred image-bearers of God, not as means to be manipulated for political advantage. I want to love and be loved. I want to belong. In the wake of Maria's death, I once again found my true home in the one, holy, catholic, and apostolic church of Christ. I'm grateful to be part of his Body.

We have been loved by the Body of Christ in our local congregation. I love our church. They have loved us well. Our church has allowed us to grieve. They have been present when we have needed them. They have given us space when we needed to be alone. Our elders and staff have worked diligently to allow me to step away from my role as a pastor in order to be a husband, a father, and a mourner. Our church has generously given to us, loved us, and walked with us.

We have been loved by the Body of Christ from around the globe. We have received cards, gifts, and messages from brothers and sisters in Brazil, Bangladesh, China, Honduras, Africa, and to the ends of the earth. People have reached out to us from across the United States. Countless strangers have contacted us to say that they are praying for our family. We have heard from hundreds of people from our hometowns, most of whom we haven't seen in twenty years. Protestant and Catholic, white and black, rich and poor, the one universal church that knows no borders, unites all races, and gives hope to all who trust in its Head. The global body has loved us well.

We have been loved by the Body of Christ in the flesh. The individuals who have sacrificed for us and touched us in our grief are far too many to name. I think of my close friend who called in the middle of the night when Maria died. He just stayed on the phone with me. I couldn't sleep. He was there. For the days and weeks and months that followed, he would regularly come over just to walk with me. And listen. He is truly a friend who "sticks closer than a brother." I think of my friend who was on vacation when Maria died but called me at 5 a.m. that morning. I desperately needed to talk with him. And he called. He was there. I think of new friends who have also lost a child. They showed up that next day and held us. And wept with us. They've been holding us and weeping with us ever since. I think of the precious couple who came to live with us that week. They took care of our children when we couldn't take care of ourselves. These are just a few of the people who were the Body of Christ to us in the flesh those first few days. If I tried to mention everyone who loved us personally and sacrificially, this post would run on forever.

32

Redeeming Pain – by Jill
(Nine Months)

A FRIEND RECENTLY FORWARDED an email to me. As soon as I saw the subject line, I knew what it was. It was a message that I had sent her just a few weeks before Maria's death. I remember writing that email. At the time I was late in my pregnancy and feeling uncomfortable and exhausted. I had had several conversations with friends who were facing difficult situations. One was dealing with family stress. One had recently had a house fire. Another was facing her infant daughter's need for major heart surgery. My friends and I were all struggling, and I stumbled across a couple of articles that touched me. I felt inspired, so I copied a few quotes from the articles and emailed them to my friends. One of them forwarded that email back to me this week.

"Instead of asking God to remove our pain, we need to start asking God to redeem our pain."[1] I had forgotten where I had seen the phrase "redeem our pain," yet it's a phrase that I've thought of many times this year. I do not want the pain to be removed. I need God to help me bear it. I need him to redeem it.

"To experience the fullness of God and walk each day filled with the richest measure of His divine presence, we must allow

1. Hayes, *Redeeming Your Pain*

ourselves to be uncomfortable with where we are and move out to where God wants us. In other words, we must find ourselves abiding in the Father making the deep places of the Spirit our constant dwelling."[1] I've never been more uncomfortable with where he has led me. Is he still with me?

I concluded my email with this. "My hope and prayer is that Christ may redeem whatever type of pain each one of us is experiencing these days to further deepen our relationship with God, further deepen our character, further deepen our relationships with one another, and ultimately bring glory to him."

I had no idea what was coming in my life. My friends were all facing much more difficult things than I was going through at the time. I had no idea how difficult it would be to face this pain; to not run from it. I do not want these dark days to be forgotten or wasted. I hope that our pain will take us deeper. I hope that God will in some way use it. I can't rush through the pain or avoid it, but I can hope that it will one day be redeemed.

1. Henderson, *Awakening Your Soul*

33

Sickness and Sleep

(Nine Months)

NORMAL PARTS OF LIFE are no longer normal. We have a couple of sick girls this weekend. Routine sicknesses no longer seem routine. Jovi has been under the weather. As she started to feel sick, I could see that she was also scared. Sickness is no longer simple. I tried to reassure her, "Jovi, even if you get a little sick, you'll be okay. Everybody gets sick. You just need to rest, and in a day or two you'll be fine."

My words are hollow. Yes, 99.9% of the time when a kid gets a virus, they recover in a few days. But the 0.1% was our daughter. Of course she's scared.

Sadie just threw up. Which means Jovi probably has the same virus. It will be a long night.

Sleep isn't easy even when all the girls are healthy. I don't sleep well many nights. Flashbacks are frequent. Once awake, it's hard to fall asleep again.

Last night Sadie, who sleeps in a small bed in our room where Maria slept at her age, kept waking up and crying out. She was having repeated nightmares. I eventually let her crawl up in bed with me to help her rest, just like Maria used to do. We both drifted off to sleep. About an hour later she screamed in terror. It was the loudest she has ever cried out in her sleep. She cried loudly in fear for about twenty seconds before I could get her to wake up and calm down. It was horrible. My heart was racing. She was fine. I wasn't. It was just a bad dream for her. She quickly fell back asleep. It was terror to me. It took me two hours to fall back asleep. Nights can be long.

34

Sackcloth and Ashes

(Ten Months)

I HAVE COME TO UNDERSTAND the importance of having specific societal norms for those who are mourning. After the death of a spouse or a child, most cultures have established standards for the bereaved. Even in the United States we're only a few generations removed from using black clothing and veils to mark those who are grieving. This may sound overly formal or inhibiting, but now I see the value. Death changes everything. It might as well change one's clothing. I wouldn't mind wearing standard clothing that publicly declares, "Death has visited my house. Everything in my life is different now."

I think standard mourning attire would be helpful for both the bereaved and for everyone else. I don't expect strangers to know the horrible thing that has happened in our lives. I know that everyone else moves on despite the fact that we haven't. I don't expect everyone to grieve with us. I don't want pity or more attention. It would just be helpful if people knew. Mourning clothes would be a sign to others that we are not normal. Some people would be able to avoid us, and I'm okay with that. Grieving is a drag. I get it. I'd rather be avoided than forced to constantly make small talk. Triviality can be painful. Or, if people decided not to bypass us, they would at least have some awareness of our situation. They would see my clothing and know that I'm mourning. And I would know that they know. Since there are no obvious signs of our grief, I find myself always wondering what to say to people. Do they know who we are? Do they know about Maria? Should I say something? Bringing up Maria's death can be awkward, but to avoid talking about her is hard too. I don't want to be the weirdo who is always forcing others into a heavy and difficult conversation, but I can't build much of a relationship with someone without sharing this huge part of our lives. Wearing obvious mourning clothes sounds easier than trying to navigate these awkward social situations.

There's another reason I desire to wear signs of mourning. Grief is not just emotional. It is physical. My body aches to hold my little girl again. I miss her in my flesh, and I feel like my body should bear signs of her loss. I've adopted two bodily reminders as signs of my grief. The first is a yellow wristband. My sister-in-law had them made after Maria died so that people could wear them on Maria's birthday. I didn't think much of it when she ordered them. It didn't seem to be a necessary thing at the time, but when they came in the mail, I put one on and haven't taken it off since. It has Maria's name, her birthday, and the day she died. It's a sign. My grief is written on my wrist.

The second is my beard. I haven't trimmed the length since Maria died. When people ask me, "How long have you been growing that beard?" I know exactly how long. When my beard was short and neatly groomed, my little girl was still alive. My world was simple and peaceful. Now my beard is long and often looks untidy, but my life feels untidy. My beard can make me look haggard. I feel haggard. It's grown long. A sign of how long it's been since she died. Far, far too long.

35

2016 – by Jill

(Ten Months)

I'VE BEEN PREPARING MYSELF for quite some time to say goodbye to 2016. I recently saw a link pop up on my social media page which was titled "Jill's 2016 in Review." It was a video montage that incorporates pictures and posts from the last year. I quickly scrolled past it. I couldn't bring myself to watch it. I hope to never relive a year like this one again. One might think that I would be looking forward to a new year, for a fresh start of sorts. Not really. I find myself facing another paradox. There is a part of me that looks with hope towards the future and to the healing that many say "comes with time." I intend to celebrate the joys of my other children as the days and years go forward. Yet I also find myself wishing I could stop the passage of time. Maria was still with us in 2016. I'm not sure I'm ready to face a year without her. I know that to remain where I am won't bring me closer to her. But memories that are still fresh will continue to fade. Our family will continue to change. Once I couldn't imagine what our family would be like without her. Soon I will not be able to guess how our family would be if she were still here.

I cannot live only in my memories. Memories will fail me. Neither can I live solely for the unknown future. I have no intentions of making any grand resolutions of self-improvement this year. I will try to face each day as it comes with as much courage and grace as is granted to me. This small pledge is as much as I can handle.

36

Foreshadowing
(Eleven Months)

SOMETIMES GOD BRINGS YOU the people you need at just the right time. Erik and Melanie have been two of those people for us. We have not been close with them for long, but through a foreboding conversation, tragedy, and shared grief, we quickly bonded with them. They have become fellow sufferers on this difficult journey.

Erik and Melanie and their children live in our community. Six years ago, their son Evan was tragically killed in a terrible accident. The accident occurred one year before Jill and I moved back to this area. We didn't know Erik, Melanie, or Evan, but we heard their story from three states away. I remember praying for them. Evan's life and death are not my story to tell, but I know that his life and death have deeply impacted countless people.

Over the past five years, I have casually gotten to know both Erik and Melanie. After running into them a few months ago, I remember telling Jill, "I really like them. They seem like our kind of people. I bet we could be pretty good friends with them." Then with my typical sarcasm I added, "But we have plenty of friends, and who really has the time for more?"

On March 1, I dropped Jill, a healthy Maria, and Sadie off at a friend's house for a baby shower that some friends were throwing for Jill, and then I loaded up Jovi, Tana, and a few of their friends and hauled them to dance practice. I ended up sitting by Melanie during the practice; her daughter is in the same class as my girls. A few minutes into our conversation I asked her when the annual Evan 5K Memorial run was going to be this spring. She spoke about the 5K, and then the conversation turned toward Evan himself. It's the first time I had ever talked with her about him. We had a deep and touching conversation. Melanie shared about Evan and about their grief. I was moved by her words. Tears came to my eyes, and I never cry. Correction: I never used to cry. I cry all the time now.

I will never forget that providential and foreboding conversation. I'm a pastor and have met with plenty of grieving and suffering people, but there are two things that Melanie shared that night that really struck me. Melanie talked about how Evan's death had changed Erik and her. They aren't the same people they were before Evan died, and some people have a hard time with that. She told me that some people just want them to be like they used to be, but they can't. Evan's death has forever changed them. There is no going back to the way things were.

There was a second thing that struck me during the conversation. About halfway through, I noticed the children dancing and all the other parents waiting while Melanie and I talked and cried. I told Melanie, "Hey, don't feel like you have to talk about this. I really don't want to make you uncomfortable and force you to cry in public."

I'll never forget her response. She said, "Tristan, you're not making me cry. I cry all the time. I like talking about my son because I love him. I don't feel awkward. Most other people feel awkward, and they just don't ask about him much anymore."

Why had I never asked Erik or Melanie about Evan? Of course they would want to speak about him. He is their beloved son. They don't want to avoid the heartbreak of talking about him because their hearts are already broken. It would be far worse for them if people like me just avoided the difficult conversation. Avoided the awkwardness. Avoided their sorrow. I can't believe I had never realized this before. Melanie wasn't afraid to talk to me about her son. I'm sure it was much more difficult to have known me for several years and for me to never once ask about him, as if I didn't know. As if Evan had been forgotten.

After dance class, I gave Melanie a hug and thanked her for sharing. She said she was grateful that we could talk because it had been a hard day. She said that God knew she needed to talk to someone that night. When I got home after dance class, the conversation with Melanie was still fresh on my mind. I told Jill about it and decided to order Melanie a copy of the book *Lament for a Son* by Nicholas Wolterstorff, the most helpful book I had read on grief. Maria came down with a fever that night. She died three nights later. The book arrived the day she died.

In the days following Maria's death, the only words I could pray were, "Oh God, help us." Jill and I took the copy of the book that fatefully arrived that Friday, and we wept and whispered the laments printed in its pages. Those laments became our words. I never did give that book to Melanie.

Early Saturday morning, a friend came over to guard against dozens of people stopping at the house to see us. I could barely breathe let alone receive visitors. "Is there anyone you want me to allow to visit?" he asked. I had a very small list of family and closest friends, and then I intuitively added, "Erik and Melanie. If they stop by, they can come see us." And they came. And they wept with us and held us. They had been mere acquaintances three days before. Suddenly they became our companions on an unimaginable and painful road.

Some have heard me talk about these events and have said something like, "See, God is in control. He was preparing you." Maybe he was, but I'm sorry if I can't take such a positive view. In my more cynical moments, my heart responds, "If God is powerful enough to send us tender friends and a book on grief to help us deal with our daughter's death, why didn't he just stop a simple virus from killing her? Where was he when we really needed him?" But my cynicism is born from my pain. It isn't really fair. The truth is that God was with us. He has been with us, and he has allowed our souls to be ravaged. We cry out, "My God! My God, why have you forsaken us?" and we also remember, "Yet, He bears our griefs and carries our sorrows; by his wounds we are healed."

Over the past months, Erik, Melanie, and their children have been a presence of grace in our lives. I told them the sarcastic comment I made to Jill about not having time for more friends. Then I said, "Sorry, you have to be our friends now. You don't have a choice. But I really wish we had never become friends. Life was far better back before we started hanging out with you guys." It's strange how sorrow can forge a friendship. In the darkest days of our lives, they have been with us in the darkness. They have known how to enter our grief because they have their own. In some way their wounds have been a salve to our damaged souls. Their sorrow reminds us that we are not alone.

Saturday was the fifth Annual Evan 5K. We attended it last year. We wouldn't have missed it this year. It was a hard day, but it was also a joy to see hundreds of people brave the cold weather to support this sweet family. They too have been well loved in their grief. Grief is a long and difficult journey. But we are not alone.

37

Comfortable being Uncomfortable
(Eleven Months)

WHEN INTERACTING WITH SOME FRIENDS and family, I get the impression that they just want Jill and me to be happy again. I get it. They want us to be better. They want things to feel normal. I can see it in their eyes. "Let's go do something fun like we used to do. Let's all be happy again!" Such interactions are awkward for me. I tend to withdraw. I suppose the awkwardness goes both ways. They feel uncomfortable not knowing how to interact with me in my grief. I feel uncomfortable with their hope to return to some sort of happy normalcy. I can tolerate the awkwardness now. It was horrible at the beginning. I distinctly remember several interactions with people bringing up politics and sports just a few days after Maria died. It made me want to throw up. How can you expect to talk to me about normal and trivial topics when my little girl hasn't even been buried yet? We can't be normal. If you want to go back to the way things were, I'm sorry, I just can't go back with you. But I'm okay that things aren't normal. I'm all right being uncomfortable.

I used to think that grieving people wanted to be comforted. Maybe some do, but I don't. I don't want comfort. I don't want pity. What I want is intimacy with my beloved daughter. I feel sorrow and pain because I long for her. There are only two antidotes that could eliminate my sorrow. One would be to have her back with us. The other would be to forget about her. The first will not happen in this life. The second would only happen if I became numb, if I ceased talking about her, if I tried to forget her, if I stopped loving her.

Sorrow and pain are the links we still have with her. If the only choice we have is between a love that aches and a comfort that forgets, we will choose aching love every time. We don't want to "be okay" with her death. Her death is not okay. But, we're okay with not being okay. Don't misunderstand. I'm not advocating that one should wallow in depression or develop a masochistic desire for sorrow. We have joy, but sorrow is part of our joy. Death is part of our life. Maria is no longer with us, but her loss is always with us. There is darkness in the midst of the light, but there is still light. I think it's these paradoxes that make some people uncomfortable, but the seemingly contradictory realities of joy and sorrow, life and death, light and darkness are now normal to us. I have a hard time feeling normal with those who just want me to laugh. I feel awkward when people just want me to be happy. But, if you have wept with me, I can laugh with you. If you've entered into my sorrow, I can find joy in your friendship. If you've walked with me in the darkness, I can catch some glimpses of light with you, even in the valley of the shadows.

38

Those She Loved

(Eleven Months)

I HAVE A DEEP APPRECIATION and affection for the people who really knew and loved Maria. Many people have loved us and reached out to us since she died. Most of them didn't know her. She was just a little kid when she died. They know Jill and me, and they love us. We're grateful. There are only a few people who really knew Maria. Those who knew her and loved her and those whom she knew and loved have become very special to us. They don't just mourn because we are mourning. They mourn because they too have lost Maria. They grieve because they loved her. They aren't just heartbroken for us. They're just heartbroken. It's easy to love those who loved our little girl.

We were recently given an album full of pictures of Maria and notes written by some friends who knew and loved her. It is a priceless gift to see pictures of her we had never seen and to hear stories about her we had never heard. It was both beautiful and extremely difficult. It took us over a month to get through it. We would turn a few pages, weep and smile, and have to set it aside. The album is the tender testimony of those who loved her.

Maria's Sunday School teacher, Doni, wrote, "Maria let me know from the very beginning of Sunday School last fall that she didn't like to color and wouldn't be participating in coloring projects. She later told me that she didn't think she was a very good colorer and that's why she refused to color. One Sunday she told me she wasn't interested in the class and she said, 'I need my space today. Just give me some space.' and I did." Have I mentioned that Maria was never afraid to speak her mind?

Several other notes were written by Chas and Carol. We've known them for about four years since they moved back to this area. Their children and grandchildren are scattered across the United States, and Maria formed a special bond with them, especially Chas. I'm not exactly sure when Maria developed such a special relationship with Chas and Carol, but they were her favorite people, and everybody knew it. Their mutual love wasn't that of family obligation. It was a friendship, and friendship is a gift.

Chas and Carol wrote, "On Sundays we used to look for each other and when our gaze met, your eyes got really big and you would tell your mommy that 'your Chas was here.' Carol and I loved having you sit with us . . . Maria was a faithful friend, one who looked forward to seeing me, and she sought me out and loved me. Her example reminds me why the life of each and every person is precious."

Maria was most playful at night when I tucked her into bed. Most nights I would tickle her and ask her questions. One playful question I asked almost every night was, "Maria, who loves you?" The answer I expected was, "Daddy loves me!" Some nights she would say, "Daddy!" or "Mommy loves me," or "Jovi loves me!" But most nights she would look at me and say matter-of-factly, "Chas! Chas loves me."

"Yes, sweet Maria, Chas does love you. And Carol and Doni and a few others who truly knew you, and we love them for loving you."

39

Property

(One Year)

SIX YEARS AGO, JILL AND I bought our first house. It's in town on a moderate sized lot on a great little street. It's nothing fancy, but we're not fancy. It's become home, and it suits us. We moved in with a toddler and a baby. We've brought three more babies into our home since then. We added a bedroom when Jill was pregnant with Lucy. The house was starting to feel a little crowded. It now feels too empty.

Owning more wouldn't make us happy. A bigger place wouldn't fulfill the deepest desires of our hearts. Stuff doesn't really matter. "What shall it profit a man if he shall gain the whole world, and lose his own soul? Or what shall a man give in exchange for his soul?" (Mark 8:36–37, KJV) . . . or his child?

I bought a second plot of land last year. Our home rests on our first. Our daughter is buried in the second. And there is an empty spot next to her awaiting Jill and me. On that day wealth and possessions will mean nothing.

We aren't owners. We are just stewards and sojourners; laborers and temporary residents for the days we are given.

"In the sweat of thy face shalt thou eat bread; till thou return unto the ground; for out of it was thou taken: for dust thou art, and unto dust shalt thou return" (Gen 3:19, KJV).

40

Good Friday Revisited
(Thirteen Months)

GOOD FRIDAY HAS BECOME THE LENS through which I can look at Maria's death. Without this day, I find her death utterly meaningless, but Good Friday reorients my distorted vision. The crucifixion of the incarnate Son changes how I see God, how I remember Maria, and how our family continues to face life without her. This holy day of suffering helps us make sense of the incomprehensible; not that I understand. Maria's death is still a mystery, but on Good Friday her death is taken up into the greater mystery of the suffering and death of the Son of God. Our suffering is united with His suffering.

I have contemplated the crucifixion many times over this past year. Every day we take up our cross, confront our pain, and stare the horror of death in the eyes. And as we look at death, we see Christ. He, too, knew suffering and death. He, too, was forsaken.

Good Friday changes even how I see my wife. I see her pain. I see her courage. I see her beauty; all through the lens of the cross. Jill has been my closest friend and companion on this excruciating and seemingly unending road, and the crucifixion continues to bolster us. I wrote her this poem on her last birthday:

On Your Thirty-Fourth Birthday

Eloi, Eloi, lama sabachthani?
In your thirty-third year
The sword has pierced your soul
Stripped and despondent
Flesh laid bare
Ye shall indeed drink of my cup
The cup of despair
Drinking the dregs of desperation
Of desolation
When they took her from us
Alone with only our tears
Where have they laid her?
Her stone bears your name
Her grave bears your heart
Her stone has not been rolled away
Eloi, Eloi, lama sabachthani?
Yet in your weeping
I see your beauty
Despite your agony
You embody grace
Your daughters have gleaned beauty
From their mother
They are beautiful
She was beautiful
Can beauty endure tragedy?
Can grace remain in horror?
Your life cries out they must
That existence is composed of these paradoxes
And beauty and grace burrow deeper
Hidden below the suffering
Eloi, Eloi, lama sabachthani?

41

Walking

(Fourteen Months)

EVERYTHING IN OUR WORLD MOVES FAST. In a little more than a century, we have gone from the horse and buggy to the SUV, from the telegraph to Twitter, from the kerosene lamp to LED lights. We have made amazing advancements in technology, and now things are advancing so quickly that the latest phone or gadget is outdated mere months after it is released. It's hard to keep up. Our families are increasingly busy, but we seem less happy. Our closets and garages are full of more and more stuff, but our lives are empty. Everything in our world is moving faster, yet most of us have never stopped to consider where we are going. We speed ahead, but we're still lost.

My fast-paced life came to a screeching halt last year. Everything stopped. It was hard to imagine how we could continue to live. The rest of the world kept speeding on around us, but our world seemed to have ended. How do you continue to live when your child is taken from you and nothing else seems to matter? Our first step in trying to answer this impossible question was literally to take a step. We walked. Lift up a foot. Put it down. Weep. Repeat. I remember wandering aimlessly with Jill those hopeless spring days. We had no destination. We didn't know how to pray.

It was hard to talk. So we walked, slowly and quietly with nothing but the sound of our crying and our weary gait.

I've intentionally avoided writing much practical advice regarding grief. Writing has been more reflecting than pragmatic. But if I were forced to give practical wisdom to those who have suffered loss, it would be this: take frequent walks. When you don't know what to do, wander aimlessly.

We've continued to walk as the days turned into months. We've logged hundreds of miles this past year. Some friends have joined us on our sorrowful path. We've been able to talk more and remember Maria as we meander side-by-side throughout our community. We grieve and share and keep walking. I sometimes find myself alone walking laps around our local school on dark winter nights while I pray and think. It's a nice lighted place to walk in the middle of the night, so if you happened to see a long-bearded, scary-looking man wandering around our neighborhood school in the dark, don't worry. It's just me.

I'm in less of a hurry these days, and I hesitate to rejoin the world at its frantic pace. I keep slowly walking while trying to remember the reason I am here. I'm doing my best to follow in the footsteps of a first century Galilean carpenter whom I believe is God in the flesh. He never ventured more than a few hundred miles from his hometown, and he walked everywhere he went. I keep thinking that if he was able to redeem the world at three miles-per-hour then it's okay for me to just keep putting one foot in front of the other.

42

Theodicy of a Three-year-old

(Fourteen Months)

SADIE CAME UP TO ME, sat on my lap tonight and asked, "Do you know why God is bad?"

"What are you talking about, Sadie?"

She repeated, "Do you know why God is bad?"

Still not knowing what she was getting at, I asked, "Why?"

"He makes us sick. That's why Maria died."

"No, Sadie, God is not bad. He is only good. He is love, and he loves us. He is not bad and doesn't do bad things."

She smiled and seemed to accept my theological correction and went back to playing with her dolls. I was left shocked by the logic and honesty of my three-year-old wrestling with faith's most difficult question. Why does God allow evil? Suffering? Sickness? Maria's sickness? Her death? Is Sadie more honest than I am about the reality of this world?

I have thought long and hard about the problem of evil, and I know that God is and must be good. I came to this conclusion long before Maria died, and I still believe it now. But some things are easier to know than to feel. I know he is good, yet there are many things I will never comprehend in my heart.

43

Embarrassing

(Fifteen Months)

I AM NOW A GUY who says really awkward things. It's embarrassing, but sometimes I just can't help myself.

I was watching the four girls at the little play area at the mall while Jill did some shopping. A young father with his wife and two-year-old daughter were just leaving when we arrived. He gave me a friendly smile and said, "Wow! Four daughters! I'm not sure whether to applaud you or feel sorry for you."

I smiled and responded, "Yeah, I know. Four girls seems like a lot. We actually had five daughters, but we lost our middle girl. So, yeah, four seems like a lot, but it feels like it's not enough for us."

Awkward pause.

Then he said, "I'm so sorry, man."

Yeah, I'm sorry, too, for dropping that bomb on you, random stranger.

44

Some Nights
(Seventeen Months)

Some nights I go out searching
When the darkness of my soul
Matches the black of the Minnesota sky
I go out looking for you
In the moments when your absence suppresses my every breath
I wander in the night
Until I find myself at your grave
One mile through the aphotic zone
From where you once lived, full of life and spunk
To where you lie, still and alone
I search in the darkness
Silent and solitary I make my vigil
Where we laid your body
I wait
But you are gone
The sun will ascend tomorrow
Rays of joy will awaken
But at night I go out searching

45

Singing Again

(Twenty-two Months)

OUR CHURCH RUNS A RECOVERY MINISTRY for people who are trying to come out of a life of addiction and brokenness. Every Friday night, twenty or thirty people show up to share, sing, and work through the twelve steps on their journey toward recovery. I don't go most Fridays, but for the past seven years I dust off my guitar once a month and show up to lead some singing. I'm not a great musician, but they're a pretty gracious crowd. We sing. I screw up. They don't judge.

A common expression on Friday nights is, "Anyone with a hurt, a habit, or a hangup is welcome." It's easy to be accepted there, but for five years I didn't really belong. I wasn't an addict. I didn't mind going, and strumming, and singing. I would attend to help out, but I didn't need to be there. Sure, I had my issues like anybody else, but I mostly had my life together.

When Maria died it seemed like all joy had forever evaporated from the desert that is my soul. It felt as if fun and frivolity, laughter, singing, and dancing would be gone forever. I stopped playing guitar. I stopped singing.

I've come to believe that there are two kinds of people in this world: those who are broken and know it, and those who are broken and don't know it. There are people whose lives are a mess and who are being redeemed, and others who pretend their lives are good but who are truly lost. I no longer live under the delusion that I have it all together.

On Friday nights, people in recovery mark and celebrate time. I never really understood this before. People earn chips as weeks and months pass. Thirty days of sobriety. Sixty days. Ninety days. Six months. One year. Eighteen months. Two years. One day at a time. Survived another day. I understand this way of marking time now. Broken people have two distinct lives. The life of addiction and the new life of sobriety. Grief also divides life in two. I mark time now. Thirty days since she died. Sixty days. Six months. One year. Eighteen months. I survived another day.

The first time I got out my guitar after Maria died was about three months later on a Friday night. There were many songs that I couldn't sing. Songs that are simplistic and naively happy. So, I chose ones that speak of suffering and sorrow and hope. And I played my guitar. And sang. And cried. We sang together with tears in our eyes, the broken and the brokenhearted. I remember thinking, "These are my people." I consider it a privilege to be numbered among the broken. I'm at ease among the recovering addicts, the abused, abandoned, and lonely. These are my people. And when I'm with them I'm finding I am able to sing again.

46

Jesus Loves Me

(Twenty-Two Months)

Our worship leader started a tradition at our church three or four years ago. Every time a new baby is born and is brought to our church for the first time, the parents and child are invited to come stand before the congregation and everyone sings "Jesus Loves Me" to the child and family. It is a tender new tradition. It is beautiful to watch a mother hold her newborn child with her husband's arm around her, often with children gathered around their legs staring up at their brand-new sibling. It's our congregation's way of welcoming a child into the body of Christ. It's our way of saying, "You belong here, little one. Here you will come to know our Lord who loves you." We've had the opportunity to sing to three children in the past six weeks. I fight back tears every time.

To be honest, I've never really liked "Jesus Loves Me." I've always thought it was overly simplistic and sentimental. I don't like many children's songs. But I've softened on "Jesus Loves Me." I don't know that I'll ever be able to sing it again with dry eyes. The final video we have of Maria is a recording of her singing "Jesus Loves Me" with her sisters just one week before she died. A dear friend was babysitting our girls that night and took the time to record a few videos, something we too seldom do. That last video is a gift. A final recording of our little girl singing that simple and sweet song. It is painfully beautiful.

I put a lot of time and thought into preparing Maria's funeral. I knew there would be a thousand or more people attending, and I wanted the funeral to honor my daughter and to speak of her beauty. And I wanted it to point us in worship to our suffering Savior; to help us see his beauty and look to him for hope. I prayerfully and thoughtfully chose all of the readings and songs. I asked several friends to help lead the service. I painstakingly composed the words that I needed to say. I spent endless hours working on that service. It was one thing I could do to love my daughter in her death.

But I didn't prepare the graveside service. It was too agonizing. We invited only a small group of family to join us at her grave, leaving the crowds behind at the funeral. I asked a friend and fellow pastor to lead the time at her grave. He was the one who baptized Maria when she was an infant, so I figured it would be appropriate if he said the final words by her graveside. I gave him no instructions. I couldn't be a "pastor" there. I was just a devastated daddy. He barely said anything. He read a brief Scripture passage and led us in prayer. Nothing more needed to be said, so he concluded by leading us in singing "Jesus Loves Me."

I choked out the words "Little ones to him belong . . . " She was never ultimately mine. She is his. A deep truth for such a simple and sentimental song.

My friend unknowingly established a tradition for our family that day. Anytime that we gather together with our girls at Maria's grave, we sing "Jesus Loves Me." I can never hold back the tears when we sing. We mutter our way through the song the best we can, often with Sadie and Lucy helping to carry us.

Two traditions. One simple song. The joy of a new child being received into the body of Christ and the ritual reminder of Maria's last song repeated each time my daughters are at her grave. Four plain words: "Yes, Jesus loves me." I cry every time.

47

The Last Sunday in February
(Twenty-Three Months)

I'VE BEEN READING THE UPPER ROOM Discourse in John's Gospel. On the day before he was to be crucified, Jesus spoke to his disciples about his coming suffering, but they did not understand. How could they? Their beliefs about the messianic ministry ended with a crown and a restored kingdom, not a cross. Jesus knew his message was cryptic and that they didn't understand. He said, "I still have many things to say to you, but you cannot bear them now" (John 16:12, NRSV). Moments later the disciples said to one another, "We do not know what he is talking about" (John 16:18, NRSV). I wonder how often our Lord speaks to us when we cannot comprehend his words. His messages are often cloaked in mystery.

The last Sunday in February 2016 was a normal Sunday. We were concluding a study on the book of Daniel. Daniel's apocalyptic vision for the exiled Jews is certainly mysterious. There are so many symbols and images in the final chapters that it's hard to decipher the meaning of Daniel's message. It's an easy passage to abuse by applying one's modern prophetic speculations onto the text. I tried to avoid that error on that last Sunday in February, and instead of pursuing wild conjecture, I spoke on the two clear overarching themes from the end of Daniel: that the people of God will suffer and that there will be a final victory over evil. "Suffering will come, but that isn't the end of the story. We're part of a bigger story in the midst of our suffering." Those were my words five days before Maria died, but how could I comprehend their meaning on that day? Looking back, I can hear Jesus whispering, "I still have many things to say to you, but you cannot bear them."

On that Sunday I read a passage by M. Craig Barnes. He tells about his father who abandoned him and his faith. His father was lost to him, but Barnes continued to hope for restoration and reconciliation. He knew that one day his father would return, be redeemed, and all would be well again. But that day never came. Barnes writes:

> "Why does that happen? Why do we spend our days banking on promises that are never fulfilled? Perhaps it happens because the promises are not confined to our expectations. God has never made himself accountable to his creatures, and his promises often appear to leave us forsaken."[1]

Those words were given to me that Sunday, but I didn't understand them. I didn't know what it meant to be left forsaken. Neither did the disciples in the Upper Room. Some messages we aren't capable of bearing. No words will ever be adequate to prepare us for all that is to come, but sometimes, as months and years pass, we can look back and catch a glimpse of a truth that was formerly opaque. We can begin to hear the words of our Lord that were cloaked in mystery and come to realize that he has been speaking to us the whole time. He has spoken. I just wasn't able to understand.

1. Barnes, *Yearning*, 25–26.

48

Hope Beyond Hope

(Two Years)

TODAY MARKS TWO YEARS SINCE our beloved Maria died. It is also a Sunday, the day of the week we gather as churches to celebrate the resurrection of our Lord. Over the past two years I have found the most comfort in the suffering of Christ. The great mystery that God descended, took on human flesh, and suffered in our midst has strengthened me in my suffering. Christ's resurrection is harder for me to imagine, just as it was hard for the disciples to imagine as they watched his broken body hanging lifeless on a cross. Who could have believed they would see him again, alive and fully restored? To imagine such nonsense is hope beyond hope. But it happened.

To imagine seeing Maria full of life again is a hope beyond hope. To one day see her walking by the river in the cool of the morning, the fullness of her humanity restored, and to hear her say, "Daddy, it's okay. Come, enter into life that is truly life. And look, Daddy, he is making all things new." Who could believe this? It is more than I can even dream.

49

Obituaries

(Two Years)

I WENT TO AN ELDERLY LADY'S funeral this week. I didn't person-
ally know her, but I know some of her family. I was moved to tears
at the funeral, but not because of the sermon or songs. It was her
obituary that touched me. Every obituary has a "preceded in death
by . . ." section. This dear old lady was preceded in death by her
parents, husband, brother, sister, other loved ones, and her great-
grandson Titus. I will never forget Titus although I never met him.
His memorial was the most sorrowful one I had ever done at the
time; surpassed only by Maria's funeral fourteen months later.

Titus's mother is a good friend. Jill and I think of her af-
fectionately as an adopted little sister. She and her husband were
expecting their first child in February of 2015. The pregnancy had
gone well with no major complications. And then I received one
of those phone calls you never want to receive. The baby was due
in just over a month, but his mother hadn't felt him move for a few
days. It just didn't seem right to her. The doctors couldn't find a
heartbeat. The umbilical cord had somehow wrapped around his
neck. Titus was stillborn at 7 ½ months. No real explanations. Just
a tragic loss. A little boy whose life was cut short.

I gathered with the family on New Year's Day, 2015, for Titus's memorial. It was an intimate gathering; just family and me. What do you say to a sweet young couple who several days before was eagerly anticipating the arrival of their first son, and then had to labor, deliver, and hold his lifeless body? I read a few laments. We prayed some psalms. I reminded them that they are now parents. While none of us ever got to know Titus, he will always be their son and they will always be his parents.

Seeing Titus's name in the obituary this week moved me with sorrow and gratitude; sorrow because of the tragedy of his life cut so short, but gratitude because he is remembered. I didn't know Titus, but I think of him and remember him. He was here. His life mattered. He is not forgotten.

I'm not quite sure why it is so important to those of us who have lost loved ones that other people remember our beloved dead, but it is important. Those who have died matter. They are loved. The world is not quite the same without them. To remember is to acknowledge their existence, their life, their death, and the giant chasm their loss has left in the hearts of those who continue to live.

I had never thought about it before this week, but those who die so young are included in generations of obituaries. They precede in death their great-grandparents and grandparents, uncles and aunts, fathers and mothers, brothers and sisters, nieces and nephews, named in obituaries for generations until the memory of their life fades away into history. And, at every family funeral from now until my funeral, I will look for Maria's name. I will see her name listed among the deceased, and cry, and remember. She was here. She was loved. She is not forgotten.

50

Two Possible Lives

(Two Years)

I CAN IMAGINE TWO POSSIBLE LIVES that look almost identical. The first life is our current family. We have had five daughters. Our middle daughter died. We still have four lovely and healthy girls and a lot of joy as well as sorrow, fear, and heartache. Our life is messy and complicated. It is depressing and hard and good and beautiful. It is the life we have been given.

The second possible life I can imagine is our current family if Maria had never been born and had never died. I can picture our life as it is currently constructed: four lovely and healthy girls, lots of laughter and joy with very little sorrow, fear, and heartache. I imagine a happy family with less mess and complication. A life without depression. I picture a simple and happy life.

And the question I've been contemplating is which life would we choose between these two possible lives? You may think it would be a difficult choice, but it is not. We would choose the first life, our actual life, without a second thought. The other life sounds easier and lighter. It is the happier of the two options, but we were never promised ease and happiness. In that life our hearts wouldn't have been shattered and our family would feel complete. That life sounds so simple, but we would never choose it at the cost of forgetting. We'll take the pain because it is the price of loving. We'll continue to suffer her death because we loved her in life.

Today we remember Maria's birthday again. She would have been six. I can't picture what she would look like or what she would be like. I can't see her in my mind anymore. Who would she be today?

The birth of your child is one of the greatest days of your life. Six years ago, this was one of those truly joyful days. Our child had been born! Tears of joy. Now, no more joyful tears. It's mostly sad, but I'm still grateful for this day. Without this day she never would have died, and our lives would be easier. If she had never been born, we never would have lost her, and our hearts never would have been broken. But I would choose this day and her life every time.

5 1

Memory

(Two Years)

I AM FORGETTING HER. I hate it. Now, over two years after her death, I have a hard time remembering her. I knew this was inevitable. The longer we live without her, the harder it is to remember what Maria was like. It's been a while since I sat down and looked at videos of her. Most days it's just too hard. When I do watch videos they spark my memory, but this just raises a difficult question. Am I really remembering her or am I forming my mental images of her on these videos? Videos are not alive. They are not her. Increasingly, the memories I have of Maria are only the mental images from photos and videos. I can't picture her in any other form. My other memories are gone. I am forgetting her.

When I was in my early twenties, I read a lot of books by Henri Nouwen. Nouwen was a Catholic priest, writer, and theologian. He was an academic who taught at Notre Dame, Yale, and Harvard, but he eventually left the prestige and acclaim of the university and moved to Toronto to live among and care for the mentally disabled. He left the best and the brightest to serve the most needy and vulnerable.

I had initially borrowed one of Nouwen's books from a library and then proceeded to purchase and read another fifteen or more of his books. During this time I was developing my own philosophy of life and ministry. I thought a lot about my future and the principles I would live by. Like most ideological young men, I thought I had some great ideas about how I would impact and change the world. There were several principles that I was particularly passionate about, and I thought I was quite brilliant for developing such profound ideas. If only everyone was so wise as my twenty-two-year-old self!

Over the next decade, I moved on to other authors and ambitions. I was married and getting more established in life, but I still believed in some of the key principles I had developed in my early twenties. I hadn't read any of Nouwen's books for a few years when I came across one of his short books that wasn't part of my collection. I had no recollection of reading this book, but as I cracked it open, it all started coming back to me. I had completely forgotten about this little gem. It was the first book by Nouwen that I had borrowed from the library many years before. It is the original book that sparked my interest in his writing, but I had completely forgotten about it. Then, I made an even more startling discovery. All of the brilliant principles that I had developed in my early twenties were stolen directly from that little book! I wasn't profound at all. I had simply taken Nouwen's ideas and then forgot that the ideas were his. So much for all of my youthful wisdom and originality!

This experience taught me something about my formation and memory. I had no direct awareness of this book. I had completely forgotten it and could not have recollected any of its content. Yet, I was deeply formed by it. I couldn't have recalled its title, themes, or anecdotes, but the ideas it contained had penetrated deeper than my conscious memory. This book continued to shape my beliefs and my character long after I had forgotten it. It formed the man I was becoming despite the fact that I had lost the memory.

I wonder if my memories of Maria are similar to my awareness of that forgotten book. As I forget more and more details of her life, it does not mean that her value is diminished or that my love for her has lessened. It simply shows my brain's inadequacy to sustain memory. All memories fade in time. My memories of Maria's life continue to diminish, but her life, the person she was, continues to shape me, deeper than I am aware. I am forgetting her. But her life still impacts all of us. She has shaped my family more than I can know or grasp. Her life mattered to all of us, even if we can't fully remember her; even if I am forgetting her.

52

Surprised by Beauty—
Another Life After Death

(Almost Three Years)

WE HAVE BEEN ANXIOUSLY ANTICIPATING the birth of our sixth child and silently dreading it. What would it be like to return to the hospital for the first time since the worst week of our lives? Lucy has been a light in our darkness, a gift of life in the valley of death, but all I can remember about her birth is the overwhelming sorrow with her entering the world seven days after her sister died. I remember pacing those hospital hallways like a ghost. And now, almost three years later, we were going back to have another child. What would it be like to return to that place, to deliver another baby where all I remember is darkness?

Life has become more normal and more manageable over the past few years. Grief has changed us, but it doesn't consume us like it once did. We've grown. Our children are doing really well. Every day there is far more joy than sorrow in our home. We laugh much more than we weep. We really are doing well.

Yet, when sorrow does come, it comes unexpectedly and can be overwhelming. We have occasional flashbacks of the moments leading up to Maria's death and of the days after she died. These memories are unbearable. I haven't written much about them because I can't. They are horrifying. When I have flashbacks to these moments, life becomes unmanageable. The darkness of depression immediately sets in, and the full weight of our sorrow suffocates us like we are drowning. These overwhelming moments have become less frequent over time, but we still have them. Certain images and memories bring them right back to the surface. This is why we were so apprehensive about going back to the hospital. To walk those sad hallways. To relive the darkest days of our lives.

But a strange thing happened. We went to the hospital last Monday to deliver our sixth child, and it was beautiful. I was expecting sorrow, but what I found was beauty and joy and hope. It was a good day. We had a few moments when we cried and remembered Maria, but even these were good moments. Her memory did not spoil the day; it reminded us of the goodness of life and the preciousness of all of our children. Her death did not overshadow the gift of the new life that has been given to us.

I was crying when Elijah Paul entered this world. Our sixth child. Our first son. I shed tears not of sorrow but tears of gratitude. Tears that see the beauty of life and know the tragedy of death. Tears that are grateful for the joy of this child.

As I held Elijah for the first time, I was overcome with one thought. "We are blessed. In the midst of all the sorrow and pain and beauty and joy, God has not forgotten us. He is good, and he surprised me with the beauty of life."

53

At Beartooth

(Three Years)

I have always longed to dwell
In mountain heights and girth
The place I ought to have been born
Where heaven meets the earth

For generations long before
Their beauty testifies
To transcendental glory
Mortal sorrow long defies

When I am most satisfied
Blissful and at peace
This is when I long the most
Where beauties never cease

But on this temporal plane I live
Where glory long evades
Where death and tragedies prevail
And happiness abates

At Beartooth

In the valley of the darkness
Death has seized my love
Forever stolen from the lowland
So I look above

For forty and six months she graced
Our home and settled hearts
Now six and forty months I look
For joy to never part

So, still I long to find my home
Above the misty peak
Though shadows cloak the holy face
A glimpse is all I seek

54

Amen

(Three Years)

MARIA WAS A DIFFICULT TODDLER. She was especially frustrating around her first birthday. At that age most children understand a lot but can't communicate much. This was true of Maria, and because she was strong-willed, she was particularly aggravated by her inability to communicate and get what she wanted. There were several months when she would moan and whine almost constantly in frustration. Dinner time was the worst. Maria knew what she liked and what she didn't like, but she didn't have the words to verbalize these distinctions. Most meals degenerated into crying and moaning. It must be hard to be a little girl with a lot to say but no words to say it.

We did try to teach her a few baby sign language signs, but she didn't really take to it. Jovi had learned a dozen or more signs when she was an infant, and that really helped with communication. By the time the third child arrived, we just didn't have the time or patience to do much sign language training. Standards drop off a lot from the first child to the third. I do remember that Maria did learn the sign for "more." She didn't use it at the dinner table, but I distinctly remember one time when I was tossing her in the air onto my bed and tickling her. She laughed and gave me the sign "more, more, more! Toss me again, Daddy!" That was about the extent of her sign language, but I'm glad she used it on that day.

Then there was the day that Maria finally spoke. Jill and I have made it a point to build healthy and consistent routines into our family life. We try to eat at least one meal together every day as a family, and we don't allow phones or screens at the table. We have consistent bedtime routines. We have also tried to develop a devotional routine. We started this when our girls were little. I would get out my guitar. We would sing a song or two, read a brief story, and pray as a family. It wasn't difficult or profound; just a simple routine. The youngest girls wander around and dance and play while the rest of us sing and pray.

On one very ordinary night when Maria was about thirteen months old, we sang and read together. Maria was wandering and dancing and playing, seemingly ignoring the rest of us. As we concluded our time of prayer, I ended with the common refrain, "In Jesus' Name . . ." and from the corner of the room we heard a squeaky little voice say, "Amen." Jill and I looked up at each other in surprise. Was that Maria? She was playing with her toys and not paying attention to any of the rest of us. I said it again more emphatically, "In Jesus' name . . ." and again from the corner of the room we heard the word, "Amen!" I did it one more time, and again Maria uttered her first recognizable word, "Amen."

Amen. "May it be so." We offer our meager prayers to the Almighty God not always knowing if he hears us. There is much I don't understand about this world. I doubt I ever will understand. His will for us is mysterious. His ways are not our ways. We pray the best we can and conclude with "Amen." May it be so. May his will be done. And we trust and hope.

It is time to bring these reflections to an end. "To everything there is a season, and a time to every purpose under heaven: A time to be born and a time to die . . . a time to weep and a time to laugh; a time to mourn and a time to dance" (Ecc 3:1–4, KJV). Grief doesn't end, but it changes. My documenting our grief needs to cease.

So, I will end here with Maria's first word. It is the same word of trust and hope that John used to conclude the last book of Scripture. After recording his apocalyptic and cataclysmic vision of this world, John concluded with a single hope. Christ will return. He will make all things new. There will be a final redemption. "He which testifieth these things saith, 'Surely I come quickly.' Amen. Even so, come, Lord Jesus. The grace of our Lord Jesus Christ be with you all. Amen" (Rev 22:20–21, KJV).

Amen. Maria. Amen. Until the day breaks and the shadows of this life flee away and I see you again. Amen.

Bibliography

Barnes, M. Craig. *Yearning*. Downers Grove, IL: InterVarsity, 1991.

Hayes, Adriana. "Redeeming Your Pain." *Just Between Us*. https://justbetweenus. org/overcoming-adversity/getting-through-hard-times/letting-god-redeem-your-pain/

Henderson, Melva. "Awakening Your Soul." *Just Between Us*. https://justbetween us.org/everyday-life/refreshing-your-soul/awakening-your-soul/

Lewis, C. S. *Mere Christianity*. New York: Touchstone, 1980.

———. *Till We Have Faces*. Orlando: Hardcourt, 1984.

The Universe Between Us by Jane C. Esther. Ana Mitchell must make the hardest choice of her life: the promise of new love Jolie Dann on Earth, or a humanity-saving mission to colonize Mars. (978-1-63555-106-8)

Touch by Kris Bryant. Can one touch heal a heart? (978-1-63555-084-9)

Made in the USA
Monee, IL
23 June 2022